LOOKING FOR THE LIONESS

LOOKING FOR THE LIONESS

A SAFARI TO MYSELF

FOOTLOOSE PUBLISHING

I'd rather be a lone lioness, roaring and free, than a caged bird without a name to call my own.

Sherry Jones, *The Jewel of Medina*

FOREWORD

I don't have a lot of memories from childhood. I vaguely remember my Mom singing Broadway tunes to me, probably because I still sing a lot of those same songs today, just a little better then Mom! Rogers and Hammerstein were big in our house, so anything from *South Pacific*, *The Sound of Music*, *Oklahoma*, or *The King and I* was fair game.

When I was a teenager, I remember playing those records (where are all those vinyls today?) constantly before I auditioned for Orange County High School of the Arts, a school that would shape the trajectory of my life. She told me she was happy I was playing that kind of music because she could sing along.

She also convinced me to add Africa to the long honeymoon my wife and I planned. We were just going to go to Europe, but I learned that Europe is for the mind, and Africa is for the soul. We enjoyed that trip so much that we decided to consciously keep adventure in our lives, and we've done a pretty good job of it. We're still thriving in our lives and always place adventure as a top priority.

I only wish that I had inherited her love of reading. My

Mom devoured books, and still does today. I've always been impressed by her vocabulary and mastery of language. I am so excited for her to unleash her knowledge and experiences into this book. From the wanderlust of her youth to the wisdom gained through her life's journey, she inspires me.

Thanks, Mom.

Matthew Morrison

MEET THE BAG LADY

You never change your life until you step out of your comfort zone.

— ROY T. BENNETT

---

*L*ike many single women, one of my greatest fears was becoming a bag lady in my old age. That specter led to many years of compulsive saving. How did I end up pushing sixty, homeless, and living out of a duffle bag?

I had lost my job during the Great Recession and my husband to divorce not long before that. A stranger was living in my home, and the rent he paid didn't even cover my condo fees and health insurance. I had no other income. So what was I doing in Africa, wandering around indefinitely with one large red duffle bag on wheels?

I guess you could say it was my son's fault. I encouraged him to go to college and study something that would get him a decent job, but he was determined to go to New York City to be an actor. As anyone who has been a tourist in New York City knows, almost all the waiters, bellhops, and bartenders in New York City are "actors." They live on peanut butter and jelly sandwiches and crash in friends' apartments, all just waiting for the right part, the big break, the ticket to stardom. Most give up and go back home to lead ordinary lives in whatever corner of the world they came from. But damn if Matt wasn't the one in a million to actually succeed, a college dropout garnering Tony, Golden Globe, and Emmy nominations for his work.

He was living his dream. I was living on unemployment, no dreams in sight. Watching him succeed through perseverance, hard work, and luck made me question my own choices.

For decades, most of my goals involved being part of a couple: where to live, how to manage child care, what to make for dinner. We went to school to finish our degrees, then worked to buy the first starter house, then moved up to the second, then the third, until we decided we each wanted our own separate house. We'd succeeded financially, but had worked so much we'd grown apart.

Once upon a time, I had been pretty adventurous. President Kennedy started the Peace Corps in 1961 and my preteen self was fascinated with the possibilities. All through high school, I dreamed of traveling to exotic foreign lands and helping the poor and unfortunate. In that pre-*Indiana Jones* era, Richard Halliburton, with his Seven League Boots, and Dervla Murphy, who bicycled from Europe to India, were my heroes. It was the 1960s and it felt like the world was being painfully but joyously reborn through music, politics, protest, sex, and drugs. American culture was shifting seismically and anything felt possible.

"I am woman, hear me roar!"

Helen Reddy's iconic song came out in 1971 and seemed to be played constantly. I was in college in Southern California and fully embraced the women's liberation movement. I never went so far as to burn my bra, but I often didn't wear one. I did wear love beads I made myself and well worn jeans. I considered myself a flower child, not a full on hippie. We embraced our friends, occasionally smoked pot, and demonstrated for Earth Day and against the Vietnam war. Peace and Love, man.

I saved my money and took my first trip around the world at age nineteen, joining the hordes of young people traveling from Europe to India. Joining the Army at the tail end of the Vietnam War promised occupational training while living out my badass MASH fantasies, with someone else paying for my travel.

I never planned to get married, but when the cute guy I loved proposed to me on top of the Empire State Building, it was hard to say no. Six months later, our love felt so overwhelming that we decided to expand our family and share our joy. I consciously gave up my wild and free life for the slippery slope of marriage, family, work, and University commitments that narrowed my options. My adolescent dreams were put to bed.

Like a dutiful wife, I kept up the home front, confident my husband was doing what was best for the family as he pursued jobs and education in cities too far to commute to and too expensive for a family to live in. In reality, we were drifting further apart every year. I often felt like a single parent, even though I technically wasn't. My introverted, laid back personality found it hard to cope with a schedule packed day and evening with my son's and my own activities. I withdrew into books and movies about adventure and romance to compensate for what was missing in my life.

The travel highlights of my 25-year marriage consisted of a road trip to Colorado and a couple of Caribbean cruises. My ex was not a good traveler, so somehow that part of me got lost. The one time I went away with a girlfriend to Acapulco for five days, my then five-year-old son came down with chickenpox the day after I left. I came home to a disgruntled husband and a tacit agreement that my solo traveling days were over.

That might have changed after we split up, but my job layoff only a couple of months later focused my goals more on economic necessity than "pie in the sky." I took a job with a previous employer and was eventually laid off again.

At this point, I was an anxious mess, feeling unloved, unwanted, and reluctant to get back in the rat race, even though I had no income and was using up my savings. Years of working as a nurse had often left me overwhelmed by death, dying, and really sick patients and families in impossible circumstances. I never was quite able to distance myself from their distress. A few times I was the last and only person to hold their hand as they died.

I just wanted to run away and start over.

"Wake up," my now-adult son, the poster boy for living your dreams, said. "What's holding you back now? You're not tied down to a job or a family you have to take care of. You can sell or rent out your condo and just go."

"But I'm old!" I said. I didn't actually feel that old, but my wandering hippie days were a distant memory. It seemed that the world had changed as well, and no longer felt like a free and easy, welcoming place. Or maybe I had just grown up and was seeing things through a more realistic lens.

"I know I need a change, but I don't know if I can handle living in a Third-World country anymore. I'll be so far away! What if I get sick? What if I get mugged and left for dead somewhere?" I said, as part of me wondered where this needy, anxious person had come from.

"It's not much different than living in Los Angeles," he said with a straight face. "The volunteer program will take care of you and give you a regular job. This is what you've always wanted to do. Just go for it!"

I grew up in southern California and had lived near a beach most of my life. It's where I go when I want to walk, to think, to ponder. Water has always been soothing to me, whether I'm in it, by it, or just listening to it. It doesn't matter if it's waves or a roaring river, just the sound of moving water calms me.

So that's where I went one day to seriously consider if this was still something I wanted to do. Live in a foreign country? Possibly with no electricity, no hot showers, no internet? What did I have to offer? I was a nurse, but for many years I had worked on a computer for an insurance company. I was good on the phone, but my hands-on patient skills were definitely rusty. Teach? Not nursing, but maybe English. Did a lifetime of speaking English qualify me to teach it? I thought back to my junior high school speech class, when standing in front of an audience made me shake so much I could barely talk. As a nurse, I felt competent with one-on-one counseling, but could I handle a whole class for an hour at a time? Would they listen to me? Or worse, would they laugh at me?

I sat on the beach and listened to the waves gently rolling in. It was a perfect day, with blue sky and a few puffy white clouds. It was a day to dream, like many days I had enjoyed there in the past, almost in this same spot. It came to me that most of those days had been in the distant past. There had been no dreams for a long time.

I remembered coming there as a little girl, walking beside my father in the sand, trying to keep up, but knowing he would never leave me behind. I remembered myself as a teenager, lying on the beach with friends and slathering baby oil all over our bodies, competing to get the darkest tan. I remembered walking into the ocean with my husband, our small son holding on to each of our hands and swinging high between us, all of us laughing happily. What happened to those people, I wondered. When did the laughter stop?

I gazed at the water and noticed something I'd never seen in all the times I'd come there. A pod of eight dolphins was traversing the shallow water along the shore not far from me. I watched, fascinated, as their bodies glistened in the sunlight every time they arched out of the water. A feeling of peace and contentment washed over me, like their slow rhythm was telegraphing me a message saying everything would be okay.

I was no longer half of a couple and needed to change my mindset and become my own person again. In the past, traveling had led to happiness and considerable growth as a person. I was no longer that young woman, but I decided that living in another country would force me to get out of my rut and find the inner strength and self-reliance that had gradually withered in my marriage. In healing myself, I might be able to help others by giving them tools to live a better life.

I considered my old dream of joining the Peace Corps. It's

6

a U.S. Government organization, just like the CIA. I had no problem representing America. I was a Veteran. I had paid taxes and been a PTA mom. But I didn't want to represent a government responsible for the deaths of thousands in recent wars and a worldwide financial crisis that slammed my personal retirement accounts, along with those of most Americans. I just didn't think people would trust me, since I didn't trust the government.

I found an alternative in WorldTeach, a non-governmental organization (NGO) founded by a bunch of Harvard students in 1986 that sends volunteers to countries around the world on one-year assignments to teach English, science, and math. The major difference is that Peace Corps covers all your expenses, while nonprofits usually charge a program fee and don't cover airfare and insurance. It was going to cost me, but I wanted to feel like I was there for the people, not the American government. And I wanted them to feel the same way.

I also balked at making the more than two years commitment that the Peace Corps required. When I was twenty, the horizon seemed limitless. At almost sixty, I was committing to a much larger percentage of my remaining lifetime. But, I reasoned, my mother had died at sixty, so anything beyond that was really a gift of time. The gift would be worthless if I hoarded it, working to buy more things I didn't need. Better to volunteer and multiply the benefits for myself and those I served.

Where did I want to go? I had traveled extensively in a previous life (before marriage), mostly on a low budget to third-world countries in Africa, Asia, and Latin America, where my dollar went further. Back then, I was young and thought I was indestructible. I blithely survived scurrying rats interrupting my sleep in Nepal, inconvenient diarrhea, multitudes of mosquito bites, questionable invitations from dicey

7

men, losing my money belt in the trackless Sahara desert, a sudden devaluation of the dollar that made changing money nearly impossible, having my clothes (my makeshift pillow) stolen from under my head while I slept on a tarp in the Congo, and listening to lions roar at night as I lay in my pup tent, dying to get up to pee. I survived all that and more, with a smile on my face most of the time.

But the Blithe Me of forty years ago was cuter, thinner, hardier, more bubbly (bubble-headed?) and gregarious. I think people would be much more inclined to help that Me than the older, heavier, grayer, more cautious present version. I prided myself on my independence back then, but looking back, most of the time I went with groups or latched on to other travelers, so I was seldom truly alone. It was much easier to hook up with other young people "on the road" back then, since it seemed that millions of us from all over the world were on the "hippie trail."

Now I have my own agenda and am not so quick to follow the crowd. I also value my privacy a lot more. Staying in a dormitory with thirty other dirty, smelly, noisy people is not my idea of fun. I like to take a hot shower at the end of the day and quietly kick back with a book and a glass of wine.

So where was my new adventure going to take me? I had had years of working to live but no longer had a job or a spouse to support me. Life in suburban America had shrunk my boundaries. Instead of looking for another job and getting back on the treadmill, I realized that I finally had the opportunity to get out of the rat race and push those boundaries out again.

WorldTeach offered a choice of several continents and many Pacific Islands. I wanted to go somewhere where I could make a difference but, like Goldilocks, I wanted it to be not too hot and not too cold. Growing up in Southern California spoiled me for weather and that wasn't a boundary I was looking to expand.

I'd had too many encounters with people trying to take advantage of me in Asia to feel comfortable living there. Latin America seemed too much like my home in Southern California. Africa seemed like the best choice, since it would *really* change the way I lived. I didn't even think about it much. It seemed that Blithe Me was back and I welcomed her.

I chose to go to Tanzania because it had a mild climate and extensive game parks, while being politically more stable than nearby countries. I wanted to see some wild animals, but I didn't want them walking to school with me. I put my living preference on the application as a mid-sized town, thinking I would probably be put in some kind of apartment with Western facilities and wild animals far away but close enough to visit.

My luggage was limited to fifty pounds and I had to be able to carry it myself. I found a wheeled Eddie Bauer duffle bag in a bold tomato red hiding behind a lot of suitcases at Sears Roebuck for half-price. My luggage color of choice leaned toward black and more black, but red would be easy to pick out at airports and too conspicuous to attract a thief. Sold! I downsized from my two-bedroom condo to that duffle bag and put everything else in storage.

"I really admire what you are doing," my son said, after he offered to put up half of the $6,000 program fee. "But living out of one suitcase is crazy."

Mr. GQ, meet the Bag Lady.

After lugging that duffle around for a few weeks, I had to agree with him, but I thought I had too much, not too little. So many people in the world would be jealous of what I had in that one bag: an Apple laptop, a phone, a camera, several pairs of shoes, two weeks' worth of clothes, a coat and umbrella. According to globalrichlist.com, I was in the top five percent in the world in terms of wealth. It sounds impressive, but I think almost all Westerners would be pretty high up on the list. The absolute poverty rate in the world has been cut dramatically since I was a teenager, but the number of people living on less than $1.90 a day (inflation obliterated the old "living on a dollar a day" poverty line) is still over a billion. My one bag represented hundreds of dollars' worth of stuff, a fortune to many.

Frequent flyer miles earned from years of credit card offers and earning one mile per dollar spent paid for my airfare. I was stopping over in London to see one of my son's concerts and he surprised me with a five-night stay in a hotel suite overlooking Hyde Park, in what was formerly the home of an Earl.

I definitely felt out of place there. Blithe Me was used to backpacker hotels when traveling overseas, not daily fresh flowers and complimentary wine and fruit. These were the kinds of hotels I usually snuck into to use the facilities, making sure not to make eye contact with the doormen. My hand-laundered clothes on the pullout line over the marble bathtub looked more suitable for camping than going to the included breakfast in the posh hotel. The staff kept putting the laundry list and bag on my bed every night when they turned it down, probably wondering why somebody staying in a place like that would be doing their own laundry.

Tanzania, home of many of those dollar-a day-or-less people, was only a nine-hour flight away. Transitioning from my luxury hotel suite in England to a $13-a-night African guesthouse was going to be a big change. I had no idea what that price would get me in Tanzania, but it probably didn't include marble bathrooms.

I just hoped cockroaches weren't part of the deal. Would the food make me sick? What would I do after I got to the airport? What if nobody met me? How would I get some local money? How would I get around? Should I just forget the whole thing and go home? No, I can't do that! Somebody's living in my condo!

My bag was packed. Time to look at the positives. Along with anxiety, there was anticipation. I felt ready for a change, and change was definitely on the horizon. The question was, would I sink or swim?

2

IN DAR

But this is Africa, so hardly anything is normal.

— ALEXANDRE FULLER, *DON'T LET'S GO
TO THE DOGS TONIGHT: AN AFRICAN
CHILDHOOD*

One of the first things I dealt with upon landing in Tanzania was discrimination. We hear about that all the time – people don't like you because you're black, white, gay, Jewish, Catholic, tattooed, female, poor, rich, old, young, or have purple hair and a beard. I get it. The world is not homogenized. What I didn't expect was to be singled out because I was American; specifically, from the United States. A person from any other country in the world could get a Tanzanian visa for fifty dollars, or even free.

"Why does it cost me so much?" I asked the immigration officer, trying not to sound annoyed after waiting in line for twenty minutes. I didn't want to irritate him so much that he put me back on the plane.

"Simple," he replied, pulling on his nonexistent beard. "You charge us $100, we charge you $100. That's the agreement."

All I could figure was that they were making a lot of money on visas for the thousands of Americans who wouldn't bat an eye at an extra hundred on top of the thousands they were paying for safaris and airplane fare, while that amount could be an effective barrier discouraging less wealthy Tanzanians from applying for a visa to go to the United States. American foreign policy at work.

After retrieving my red duffle bag and going through customs, I looked around and noticed a sign with my name on it. The next thing I noticed was a beautiful smile directly above it. It belonged to a slim, blond woman in her late twenties wearing what I came to know as her standard long-sleeved top and long skirt, considered professional attire in a Muslim country where you weren't supposed to show your shoulders or your legs. She introduced herself as Ashley, the Director and sole employee of WorldTeach Tanzania.

"You are going to love it here!" she said. "But it takes a little getting used to."

As we walked out of the building, the heat and humidity hit me like I had just walked into a wall. I really was a long way from London. Just like in London, they drove on the left and the traffic was horrible. But as our taxi wove in and out through the maze of traffic, I realized it was much more chaotic. There were very few traffic lights, stop signs, or crosswalks, so the driver played a game of chicken at all the intersections. Aggressive driving was the key, so polite Londoners would be at a severe disadvantage. I had to close my eyes as we came to roundabouts and squeezed in between much bigger trucks and buses.

Dar es Salaam ("Home of Peace") is a city of over four million people, more than Los Angeles. It was a fishing village until the German East Africa Company built a station there in 1887. The British took over in World War I and constructed some substantial buildings in the center of the city before the country gained independence in 1961. Most of the housing is in "informal settlements," which I take as a euphemism for unplanned. I saw mean shacks with straw roofs interspersed with more sizable houses that reflected the homelands of the Arabs, South Asians, and Europeans who settled there.

We drove for about an hour through the chaos, passing hundreds of roadside stalls set up by entrepreneurs to sell clothes, produce, tires, tools, and almost anything else you could think of. Some people just piled a lot of old clothes a blanket on the ground and waited for business. Often, enticing smells of roasting meat or baking bread permeated the surrounding air. The cacophony of traffic, honking horns, and shouts of the people selling their wares was loud and constant.

Finally, we got a respite from the noise after we turned onto a dirt road that led to the Msimbazi compound, the gated Catholic conference center the new volunteers would be staying at for the next week. The compound was like a small village, with churches, several canteens, indoor and outdoor meeting venues, schools, and living spaces. We stopped in front of a two-story boxy gray building.

"We will have this whole building for ourselves," Ashley

explained. "The thing is, the other volunteers aren't arriving until tomorrow. Will you be okay here on your own?"

"What about you?" I carefully asked, trying to clarify what "on my own" meant.

"I live in town," she said. "But let me introduce you to the matron here."

I was glad I wouldn't be left totally alone, but "matron" sounded like somebody in charge of a jail. I grabbed my duffle bag and we walked to a small office opposite the entry door. Ashley introduced me to Masumi, a short, sturdy woman in a turban, who grinned at me with a gap-toothed smile.

"*Jambo*," I said, practicing my limited Swahili for the first time. I had heard the word in Hollywood movies and it wasn't until much later I was told that only foreigners used it.

The grin got wider. "Hello, and welcome," she said, inclining her head slightly. I later found out that was about the extent of her English vocabulary.

The taxi was waiting outside, so Ashley left to go back to her rented house in town. As soon as she left, the exhaustion and gritty feeling resulting from a full day of traveling from foggy London to tropical Dar es Salaam caught up with me. I found my room, swiftly stripped and threw my clothes on the bed, then went into the bathroom to turn on the hot water in the shower.

The exposed pipes made a banging noise, but nothing came out. I stared at the faucet and waited. Nothing. Not even a drop of water. I could ignore the beetle racing across the wall toward the open window, but *I needed a shower! Now!*

I put my sweaty clothes back on and went downstairs to find Masumi. I think I was able to make her understand what the problem was, but I couldn't understand what she was telling me. I don't remember cussing and tearing my hair out, but I probably wasn't being my most diplomatic. Masumi had lost her grin long before she called Ashley to translate.

"*Habari*," Ashley answered cheerfully, that one word of greeting promising a friend in the wilderness, there to banish all my problems. I briefly told her the issue and had her speak with Masumi. After a lot of muttering in Swahili, Masumi handed the phone back to me.

"They don't have running water after 2 p.m." Ashley explained. "You'll have to wait till tomorrow to take a shower."

"You've got to be kidding me," I groaned, feeling every inch of the sweaty, rank-smelling clothes I had been wearing for almost twenty-four hours. "What time in the morning?" I asked, picturing how frustrated I would be if I tried to turn the water on too early and it still didn't work.

"Six a.m. The other volunteers aren't getting to the airport on the group flight from the States until nine, so we'll be at the compound around ten or eleven. Go to the canteen for breakfast."

"Okay," I replied, feeling calmer now that I knew I would get clean before too long. I wasn't worried about finding food because I had seen the canteen on the way in. "Thanks, I'll see you tomorrow."

"*Kwaheri* (goodbye)," she replied, hanging up.

Back in my room, I turned on the ceiling fan and exchanged my sweat dampened clothes for a clean night-gown, thinking that between my dirty body and the humidity, I would have to wash that tomorrow, too. I turned over in bed and let out a big breath and my problems with it. Sleep came quickly.

The next day I woke up early and showered. The water wasn't hot, but the coolness sluicing down my grungy body

16

felt wonderful. I hand-washed my dirty clothes and hung them up around the louvered window. I had learned on previous trips that when you are living out of one suitcase, you should keep as many clothes as possible clean so you don't have to worry about your wardrobe when you get busy. It was probably the last free morning I would have for a while, since the other volunteers would arrive soon.

By this time, my body was craving coffee. I walked to the canteen and was surprised to see that I was the lone customer in the outdoor patio adjacent to the cooking hut. I sat down at a long metal table covered with a white plastic tablecloth, facing a wall of bright red bougainvillea and scented white roses. The server rolled her blue and yellow apron up in her hands as she sauntered over to me.

"I'm Mama Sam. Whatcha want 'ta eat, mum?" she asked, leaning her white turbaned head to one side and eyeing me speculatively.

"I'd like coffee with milk and a menu, please."

"Ya can't have no menu," she said, her eyes narrowing.

"Am I too late for breakfast?" I asked, hunching my shoulders and thinking maybe that was why no one else was there. My coffee craving was howling.

"No late, but no menu."

I finally figured out that there was no printed menu, as they served the same thing every day. Eggs were scrambled unless you specifically asked for poached or fried. Toast was always white bread with jam and butter. Fruit was whatever was on hand, usually melons, bananas, mangos, or papayas. Milk and water came in pitchers.

There were tea bags, but I never saw brewed, flavored, or decaffeinated coffee the whole time I was in Tanzania. Coffee is their largest agricultural export but only seven percent stays in the country, according to the Coffee Board of Tanzania, and all of that must go to the makers of instant coffee. I am not a coffee snob, but I never would have touched the stuff in America unless I was desperate. With no alternative, instant coffee tasted pretty good with a lot of hot milk. I drank it almost every day after that.

When I got back to our building, I saw a parked van surrounded by piles of luggage. A few white people stood on the porch talking. I surmised that the other fourteen volunteers had arrived.

"Hi," I said, smiling as I walked over to meet the strangers I would spend the next few weeks with, learning how to survive and thrive in our new communities before we scattered to assignments all over the country. "I'm Mary and I come from California. How was your flight?"

"Long," groaned a tall girl with waist length blond hair I came to know as Cindy. I had only come from London, while many of them had one or more flights before they boarded the group flight from Washington, D.C., to Tanzania, with a two-hour stopover in Europe. Part of me felt bad that I had missed the initial bonding-in-our-misery experience that had probably already resulted in some pretty tight friendships, but I didn't envy them the twenty-plus hours of traveling.

After more introductions, the rest of the group came out to get their luggage. They had been inside with Ashley getting room assignments. Most were paired with roommates, but my room remained private. I don't know if that was because I was there first or if it was a concession to my age, since, at fifty-nine, I was the oldest person there.

Most were in their early twenties. WorldTeach programs require a college degree, and many of the volunteers had just graduated and wanted some life experience before going on to jobs or to medical or law school.

Others were looking for validation of life choices or

"something more." Megan, age thirty-two, described herself as a burned-out computer engineer. Gretchen, an accountant, had just finished a year with WorldTeach Marshall Islands and didn't feel ready to go home. Katie had taught at a school in South Africa for two years and was debating whether to go back to South Carolina to get her Ph.D. Rachel, age forty-five, lived in my hometown of Santa Monica and was the closest to me in age.

We came from eleven different States and Canada. The geography varied, but all of us were Caucasian.

There were only two males in our group of fifteen. Looking back, I found this pretty consistent with my experience of volunteers and backpackers in Africa. Maybe the guys were in the back of beyond where I never saw them, but judging from the people I met in hostels and the gathering places of NGO and Peace Corps workers, women were the majority in "adventure" mode. I'm not sure why this surprised me. In its infancy, sixty-five percent of Peace Corps volunteers were men. Now that percentage is reversed. The next Indiana Jones-type movie should definitely be about a woman.

Ashley held a short introductory meeting, but most of the group were dead on their feet. I could see heads bobbing on chests and even heard a gentle snore in the back of the room.

"I can see that I'm wasting my time," Ashley said with a rueful smile, as she started putting away her notebook. "Let's meet at 9 a.m. tomorrow, after breakfast." The other volunteers, at least the ones who were still conscious, were quick to agree.

The rest of the day was spent relaxing, but the blare of disco music kept me up from 6 p.m. till about 1 a.m. The religious compound hosted several weddings a week. I don't know if I had arrived on an off night the day before or if I was so tired I actually slept through the racket.

During my stay, I saw many large groups of mostly black people, dressed to the nines in suits and formal gowns. They bunched up in front of the compound's several venues, where small round tables with white tablecloths were set up. Sometimes the facility hosted three weddings in one night, and only the color of the centerpieces and bows on the metal folding chair covers differed. The loud music persisted, except for short breaks when an equally booming voice praised the bride, the groom, and the attendees over a loudspeaker.

The music finally stopped sometime after midnight but was replaced by the annoying high-pitched drone of a couple of mosquitos continuously diving around my mosquito net. Eventually, I nodded off but was jerked awake by someone shouting over a loudspeaker nearby: "*Alaaaaahhhhhhhhhhhh…*" The muezzin was calling the faithful to prayer, an event that happened every morning at 5:45. I must have been really out of it to sleep through it my first night, because the speakers on top of the nearby minaret sounded louder than the DJ's.

It is not unusual in Tanzania to find a mosque next to a Catholic church. The population is about evenly divided between Christian, Muslim, and homegrown religion followers. The first President after independence from colonial powers in 1961, Julius Nyerere, failed economically with his socialist policies, but *Ujamaa* (unity) brought improved health, education, and life expectancy.

Forced relocation of students and sometimes whole villages diminished the tribal strife seen in other countries, as people came to identify themselves as Tanzanians before any tribal or religious identity. Nyerere is still revered as the

Father of the Country, just like George Washington but with a Maoist bent.

~

Our first week in Tanzania was spent getting cell phones and internet modems, learning how to use local transportation, and generally orienting to the country. We went as a group to the U.S. Embassy. There was no physical sign of the 1998 bombing by Islamic terrorists that killed eleven people, but our passports were carefully screened. Cell phones, purses, backpacks, and water bottles were temporarily confiscated before we passed through a metal detector into the main complex. Secretary of State Hillary Clinton had been there the week before to help celebrate the fiftieth anniversary of the Peace Corps. The Ambassador, a former WorldTeach volunteer, was very supportive of us.

The Embassy nurse gave us an eye-opening talk about all the infectious diseases we could catch there. Ninety percent of the country is in a malaria zone, so she talked about prophylaxis and demonstrated how to do a home malaria test, which involved a drop of blood and reagent on a test strip, much like a diabetes test. I had tried to purchase one of these in the United States and couldn't find a place that sold them. In Tanzania, you can get one at any drugstore. A lot of the volunteers would not live near a drugstore, much less a hospital, so the purchase of home test kits was recommended.

The head of security told us what to avoid, which was pretty much everywhere and everything. Listening to him talk of wild animals, poisonous snakes, terrorists, insurgents on the borders, rapists, muggers, crazy drivers, and the current drought, it felt as if we would never get out of the country alive. But thinking about it, I could have given that same speech about Southern California, substituting cougars for lions and drug runners for border insurgents.

In counterpoint, Ashley arranged for us to meet some of her Peace Corps friends, in town for the anniversary celebration, for dinner at a nearby restaurant. They were teachers, farmers, foresters, and technology workers. Most of their living situations were pretty primitive, some with no running water or electricity, but all seemed to like their jobs. I had some concern talking to Karen, a teacher who lived in a hut in the countryside with an oil lamp for light and a river to bathe in. She had signed up for a second term, "to see my kids graduate." I was bothered that, although she said she was twenty-six, her leathery skin and bagged eyes made her look at least ten years older. Considering my advanced age, what would I look like in a year?

The next day, we teamed up with local University students, who had volunteered to show us around town in exchange for a chance to practice English. Alicela, a 22-year-old finance major with huge eyes and a smile to match, joined Katie, Jacob, and me.

Our first challenge was getting on the local bus, or *dalla-dalla*. I was already freaked out by the traffic. The Embassy had told us that the chance of getting killed in a traffic accident in Tanzania is more than double that in the United States. In Dar, it's probably quintupled.

The *dalla-dallas* looked like ancient mini-buses. Numerous dents and scratches advertised their road warrior status. They were independently owned, unregulated, and had no apparent schedule or numbering system.

"Look for '*Poste*' on the front, and it will take you to the downtown Post Office," advised Alicela.

I noticed that a lot of the *dalla-dallas* said "*Poste*" but the second word varied.

"How do I know which one to take to get back?" I asked.

"It's too confusing," she said, shaking her head. "Take a taxi."

So much for learning how to get around Dar.

We walked toward a *dalla-dalla* that had a crowd of people clambering to get on. People did not line up, but all tried to get on at once, and there didn't seem to be a limit to how many could board. It was apparent that we weren't all going to make it, so we waited for a second *dalla-dalla* and made sure we were in the front of the crowd when it stopped.

Besides a driver, each *dalla-dalla* had a conductor who took money at the door. He was very adept at making change, and his hands seemed to move continuously at lightning speed between the stack of paper bills in one hand and the coin sorter on his belt. We were crammed in like sardines and had to stand during the ride, hanging on to the luggage rack as we tried not to breathe in the pungent human fragrance around us. The advantage was that the mass of people blocked my window view of our many near-death experiences, although I felt the swerves and sudden stops as I struggled to stay upright.

"Mind your things," called Alicela from where she stood near the back of the bus. I didn't know if that was meant more for us or to warn potential thieves that we weren't solo tourists ripe for the picking.

We made it downtown and walked around for a while viewing the waterfront, churches, and government buildings. "Walked" is the wrong word, as there were so many people that it was more like getting around an obstacle course. I don't know why you can walk in New York City with tons of people and go in and out of the flow with no problems. In Dar, there seemed to be no order to the flow, as people ambled in both directions with no preference for the right or the left side, often stopping abruptly to chat. Our faster walking pace led to several near collisions.

Suddenly, it started to rain. Rain in Tanzania is not soft or gentle, but a deluge. When it rains, it comes in a torrent. People don't bother with umbrellas, but duck under the nearest overhang and wait it out, besieged by what sounds like hundreds of thundering hooves on the roof. The rain doesn't last long, and you go about your business until you repeat the process again a short while later.

We managed to get undercover before getting totally soaked. After the rain let up, we sloshed through the puddles to a nearby restaurant Alicela suggested. It was not what I expected, as it was not a regular building, but a large roof of skinny logs topped by sheet metal, with log pillars holding it up.

The meal was set up buffet-style on a long metal table. I picked up a ceramic plate and a fork, the supply of which seemed to be constantly recycled. As people finished their meals, they took their dishes to a man who washed them in a bucket of soapy water, dipped them in rinse water, and stacked them wet on a table next to him. A server came by and carried the wet dishes to the stack at the beginning of the line.

"What is this?" I asked Alicela, as I stood in the buffet line staring at a pile of white dough on my plate.

"*Ugali*," she replied. "We eat it with almost every meal. It's maize flour and water. You know, from corn."

"OK, I want to try everything," I said. Later I amended that with "once."

The next two dishes in the line were more recognizable: meat stew and a bean and tomato dish. We also bought bottles of water to drink and found an empty table on the side of the room.

"Here is what you do," Alicela said, as she pinched off a piece of her *ugali*, rolled it in her hand, then stuck her thumb in the middle of the ball to form an indentation. "Fold it around the food and pick it up and eat it." She plucked a piece of meat from her stew and popped it quickly in her mouth.

I picked at a piece of the moist dough and nibbled it. "This doesn't taste like anything."

"Eat it with the stew," she said.

"OK, easy," I said, as juice from the stew dribbled down the front of my shirt. I decided then and there that I didn't really like *ugali* because it had no taste and the texture was kind of gross. I picked up my fork and ate the rest of the meal. Meanwhile, Jacob and Katie dug in with their hands and seemed to enjoy it.

The rain started again. The metal cover on the log roof magnified the thundering sound and we couldn't hear ourselves talk. The restaurant had no walls and the rain blew in and soaked us. Too late, we understood why that was the only empty table when we came in.

Life is about learning to adapt, but I can live without *ugali*.

We talked Alicela into taking us to the Medical and Technological University, where she was a student. We hopped on a couple of three-wheeled motorcycle carts. These seemed even more dangerous than the *dalla-dallas*, but the drivers stuck to less traveled roads and even went on and off the sidewalks to avoid traffic. Still, it was not for the faint of heart.

The University consisted mainly of several long concrete block buildings. We could see instructors and their classes through the windows as we walked toward a smaller building that housed the Student Union. Alicela told us that eighty percent of the population of Tanzania lives on farms, and most of the students were like her: the children of farmers, determined to make better lives for themselves and their families.

"When I was going to University in the United States, a lot of students considered it a four-year party," I told a group of students we met.

"In our country, the whole family has to struggle to send a child to University," said Kametha, a tall, beautiful girl with long eyelashes and intricately braided hair that hung around her shoulders. She hoped to become a doctor but was anxious about the long road to get there.

"School is expensive, and the scholarships go mainly to the children of government workers. If we don't graduate, we will be back on the farm and our families in debt for the money already spent. I will have no way to pay them back."

"Sometimes I think we traded wedding gowns for graduation gowns and debt," said Alicela. Her laugh turned into a frown as she added, "I worry that I am putting my family in a terrible situation, but the opportunities ahead of me if I can graduate promise me a life I could never have on the farm. Time will tell if we made the right decision."

Alicela showed us her dorm room, which consisted of two bunk beds and one small desk under the window between them. The space was so tight that two of her roommates had to leave the room so we could enter. Outside again, the main difference I could see from American dorms was that almost every window had a lot of laundry hanging from it. I never saw a washing machine my entire time in Tanzania. You could hire someone to do your wash for you, but it was still done by hand in a bucket of water and hung out to dry.

After walking us to the main road, Alicela called a taxi and hugged all of us goodbye. "I'm glad you have come to our country to help us," she said. "We want to be part of the world."

Tired and a little overwhelmed by this new world we had flown into, we rode the taxi back to the compound in near silence that seemed to drown out the cacophony that swirled around us.

3

ORIENTATION

You never know what's around the corner. It could be everything. Or it could be nothing. You keep putting one foot in front of the other, and one day you look back and you've climbed a mountain.

— TOM HIDDLESTON

"*M*añana time" is alive and thriving in Tanzania. Restaurant servers could take two hours to get to your table, and if someone told you the waiter would be back "in a while," it could mean two minutes or two days. They didn't even bother to post bus schedules, as buses came "when they were supposed to." I waited an hour for a bus and then two of the same route came at the same time.

Our group of punctual and optimistic Americans lined up with our baggage by 8:45 a.m. in front of the hostel to board a bus that was supposed to leave at nine and take us to our training compound near Lushoto in northeast Tanzania.

"*Safari*" means "journey" in Swahili, and we were looking forward to our first view of the country outside of the craziness of Dar es Salaam.

We waited... and waited... and waited some more. The hostel staff had no information about the bus. All eyes were on the taxi that rolled up as Ashley, our supervisor, slid out of it. She held up her hands, whether to gain attention or for protection, I wasn't sure. Her green eyes looked a little wary and her posture a bit hunched as she walked over to us.

She looked around to make sure she had everyone's attention before saying, "The transportation manager at the bus company had some 'personal issues' and never arranged our bus. I talked to his boss and he said he would get a car for us this afternoon. Go to the canteen and get some lunch, then meet back here in an hour."

After waiting so long, it felt good to get up and move and eat. Ashley never explained how we would all fit in one car with our luggage and I didn't ask. In any case, the car never showed up. After more frantic phone calls, Ashley finally gave up. Luckily, no one had booked our rooms so we piled back into the hostel for another night, with the promise of a bus at 9 a.m. the next day. It was a long night because there were several weddings taking place in the compound and loud, blaring disco music came from several directions through the wee hours. I felt like I had just gotten to sleep when the muezzin started up with his highly amplified 5:45 a.m. call to worship for the Muslims. "*Allahu Akbar... Allahu Akbar...*"

Fifteen sleepy Americans shuffled out of their rooms, dragged their luggage outside onto the dirt road, and lined up for a bus that never showed up. The usually calm Ashley became more agitated and finally got in touch with the driver around 11 a.m. What sounded like some harsh words in Swahili ensued before she turned to face us.

"The driver said he was at the Ministry of Education trying to get gas money for the trip," she explained. "I requested the bus a week ago, but I can't say this is atypical. Just chalk it up to TIA. Just say it and let it go or you'll never survive here."

TIA, or "This is Africa," became an oft-used phrase in the coming months. It encompassed swearing, resignation and surrender to things I had no control over.

The bus finally showed up five hours late and we lost no time piling in with our stuff. We left too late to complete the six-hour trip before dark. Ashley and the driver were having increasingly tense conversations about driving the last two hours up winding mountain roads in darkness. Safety over-ruled budget concerns, and we ended up staying at a pretty nice Western-style hotel overnight.

As we were getting assigned our rooms, Diana, a slim brunette from Arkansas, complained of fever and stomach upset. Ashley asked her if any mosquitoes had bitten her. Diana's face paled as she nodded and whispered, "Malaria."

By this time, they had lectured us so many times about taking prophylactic pills that we had a real fear of getting the disease. I rolled my eyes as everyone seemed to take a step back from Diana, like the dead mosquito that had bitten her would jump onto them. It reminded me of taking care of AIDS patients in the mid-1980s, when everyone wore full isolation gear and all the patients were expected to die, because that was the only outcome we had ever heard of at the time.

I had purchased a malaria test kit in Dar and Diana agreed to be my first patient. Ashley put us in the same room, since everyone else was shying away from her. Diana had only been in Africa for a week, so it was doubtful she would test positive. But it was nice to use some of my nursing skills and give her some reassurance. She slept well and seemed fine the next morning.

I gained a lot of respect for Ashley's organizational skills when she got us on the bus and rolling by 6:30 a.m. Most people went back to sleep, but those still awake had our first sighting of African wildlife, two grizzled and tired looking baboons that stared at us through red-rimmed eyes from the side of the road. It was a pretty pathetic sight, but that didn't stop everyone from frantically taking pictures before the bus got too far away.

We were soon off the tarmac and on steep, winding dirt roads with deep ruts from recent heavy rains. I had my doubts that the long bus could stay in one piece, as the wheels repeatedly fell into cavernous pits, but the driver somehow managed to slowly grind our way out of them.

Besides anxiety about the road, everyone was starving since we hadn't eaten yet that day. I had forgotten Rule #1 of travel: always carry water and a snack. We finally reached the cluster of buildings that would be our home for the next two weeks. We piled out of the bus and Sabine, the manager of the compound, welcomed us with a smile, a hot English breakfast, and coffee. She had originally come to Tanzania from Germany to work a short-term contract as a nurse, but fell in love with the country and her Tanzanian husband and had now been there for several years.

The compound was in a beautiful valley surrounded by green mountains. There were four sleeping cottages with four beds in each, so our group of fifteen plus Ashley, the World-Teach coordinator, just fit.

We had hot running water, which was a big improvement over the cold showers in Dar es Salaam. The problem was the limits of the water tank and the generator that heated the water. I could probably add to that the love of fifteen Americans for hot showers, uncomprehending that they were not dealing with the unlimited flow of a public water system. The hot showers were doomed to come to an end.

The difference between hot water and hot *running* water is the difference between a bucket bath, where you stand up and continually reach down to dip a cloth in rapidly cooling water, and a shower where you close your eyes and dreamily enjoy steaming water sluicing over your body in a constant stream.

Sabine made it known that our Western ways of frequent bathing and charging multiple electronics were taxing the generator and the water supply, which was trucked in from a local water source. If we ran out of water before the next scheduled delivery, her husband had to go to town and purchase huge ten-gallon buckets of water. We ran out pretty quickly, so he put one bucket in each bathroom as a visual cue to remind us that was all the water we had to bathe and flush the toilet for a while. He refused to lug more buckets from town.

Fortuitously for the rest of us, the younger girls, who seemed to take a lot of time in the bathroom and use a lot of water for hair washing, all shared the same cabin, along with Ashley. Hopefully they worked the problem out among themselves. I had no doubt that Ashley gave them some pointed tips on how to curb their resource consumption to better survive in Africa.

I was happy to be sharing a cabin with Katie, who had just finished teaching for two years in South Africa, and Gretchen, who had just completed a year with WorldTeach in the Marshall Islands. Noah, a recent college graduate and one of the two men in the program, rounded out our residence.

Sabine told us that only sixteen percent of the country's population had electricity and what they did have was not dependable. The compound had scheduled blackouts for a few hours at a time to save power, but it still could go out at any time. We learned to carry a flashlight even in the daytime since night dropped precipitously near the equator and there were no outside lights to guide us. When the power was on, the multitude of phones, laptops, and various other devices (yes, some people brought hairdryers) sapped the energy supply. Charging devices was restricted while meals were being prepared so the ovens wouldn't lose power before the meal was ready. We were happy to comply with that rule so we could enjoy the delicious food.

Meals were largely vegetarian and consisted mainly of rice, chapatis (fried Indian flatbread), beans, cabbage, mangos, papayas, oranges, and bananas, but there were occasional surprises of German sauerbraten or barbecued chicken. We had three meals a day, plus afternoon tea. The head cook, Mama Danny, was often seen working outside the cooking shed with her baby, Danny, strapped to her back. Women take the name of their youngest child, so Sabine was known in town as Mama Deborah. I couldn't imagine having ten children and changing my name every year.

Ashley and Sabine had their hands full trying to mold fifteen spoiled, entitled Americans into self-sufficient, savvy individuals who could survive a year in rugged conditions. We each had to take a turn helping out for our "cooking lesson" because we would be responsible for providing our own food. Some of the teaching assignments were considered "challenging," with no electricity or running water. I think Ashley was checking us out to see who could meet the challenge before she assigned us to our permanent posts.

For our cooking lesson, we made *ugali,* which I had

already decided was not going into my collection of treasured family recipes. I learned to grind corn standing up, using a huge bludgeon to pound it into pieces. I then mixed the cornmeal with water and flour in a huge vat and kneaded it to the proper consistency. We prepared food in large quantities, so both of these tasks made my arms feel like they were going to fall off. Another reason to forego *ugali*.

One day we were divided into teams of three and sent to the local market. Each team was given 5,000 shillings (about four dollars) and a shopping list consisting of mangos, tomatoes, onions, flour, and beans, with amounts unspecified. The market stalls each carried only one or two of the things on our list, so we would have to shop around, find out what things cost, and learn how to bargain.

We compared how much we got for what we spent with the other teams when we got back to our residence. After careful shopping, my team had been surprised to discover that we had the majority of our money left. We used the remainder to buy two kilos of beans, thinking it prudent to buy something that would not spoil. One team favored tomatoes, thinking they got a good deal on them. The young girls came back with twenty mangos and a little of everything else. "We just ran out of money," they explained.

"Be careful," warned Gretchen. "Eating too many mangoes can make you sick." She was speaking about an unhappy memory from her Marshall Islands assignment.

The last team to report consisted of the two guys, who had banded together, and Katie, who had lived in South Africa for two years. Nobody expected them to win, thinking that women had a natural edge when it came to shopping, but they beat the other teams hands down, getting more of everything at better prices.

"Men are just better negotiators," bragged Noah. Katie,

the only female on the guys' team, didn't say anything but there was a definite smirk on her face. I suspected that she had done a lot of shopping during her time in South Africa, giving her a definite advantage in the challenge.

Most of our days were spent in the classroom, where Ashley provided instruction on how to teach English. Sabine taught us Swahili, the common language in Tanzania, which might not be the same as the native language of our yet-to-be assigned village. Mr. Samy, a local school teacher, shared information about Tanzania and its culture.

Occasionally we took long hikes in the surrounding mountains, where long-range views gave us a better sense of the beauty and awesomeness of Africa. The breathtaking sunset views across the seemingly endless landscape made me feel a deeper connection with the land and sky, like Africa was seeping into my bones.

~

Right before "graduation," we each had an overnight home-stay with a local family. My hostess, Lightness, worked at the local hospital as a psychiatric and HIV/AIDS nurse, so her maid, Sanitaa, picked me up at the compound. As we walked about thirty minutes to the house on the other side of the valley, we talked about the town and the people who lived there. She was a childless widow and happy to have work to help support her after her husband died in a farming accident.

"I like being independent," she said. "Without a job, I would have to return to my family home. I would be like a free maid for them. Lightness is also a widow, and she treats me with respect and pays me."

I was given tea while I watched her prepare dinner on the

clay stove, located in an interior patio. I sat comfortably on a small ledge while she squatted in front of the stove for so long it made my legs ache just watching her.

"Does squatting in that position for so long bother you?" I asked.

She smiled and laughed. "No, of course not. We sit this way all the time." I pictured the squat toilets I had used in Asia, but I knew this house had a regular Western bathroom. I had checked.

A middle-aged black woman in a long gold print dress with black trim and a green head wrap showed up at the outside entrance to the patio and started talking to Sanitaa. After some back and forth conversation, the newcomer turned to me and said, "*Habari*. I am Lightness and I am happy to meet you. Welcome to my home."

"*Asante sana*," I responded, using my limited Swahili to thank her for her hospitality. "I hope you had a good day at work."

"Yes, it was a good day," she replied. "I delivered twin babies, so that was a double blessing to their family. Maybe tomorrow I will take you to visit the hospital."

"I would love to see the hospital. I am a nurse in my own country."

"That is wonderful," she said. "We are sisters. Would you like to go to church now?"

"Of course," I replied. "I want to learn about your country and see how you live, if you don't mind showing me."

She smiled, which seemed to be her usual facial expression, and explained that "church" for today was the Friday night Pentecostal prayer meeting. The next day we would go to her regular Lutheran church.

We had to walk the long way on the road after I apologized that I doubted I could manage the "short cuts" she normally took, which involved scrambling up steep dirt hill-sides with no handholds. A neighbor standing on top of one of the mini-hills that might as well have been a mountain to me started conversing with Lightness in their native language. Maybe I'm paranoid, but I thought they were probably joking about how lazy and inept Americans were. She just turned to me, smiled, and waved me on down the road.

The church was a squat whitewashed concrete building with a wooden cross above the front door. We entered what looked like someone's living room, with rows of chairs arranged in a horseshoe with one open end. Lightness intro-duced me to some of her friends, who smiled and nodded their heads. They didn't all speak English so she had to trans-late for me. I was the only white person in the room.

A short, slender man in a brown suit and tie walked to the front and started the service, which was mostly in Swahili. It was very mellow, with readings and hymns. All of a sudden, I heard a door banging and looked up to see a seven-foot-tall black man in a tight mustard colored suit and red tie. With his height, baldness, and handsome looks he resembled an NBA player. He looked around before sitting down in a nearby chair. Nobody seemed to take special notice of him.

The reading continued and I thought he was asleep, but apparently he was just gearing up for his fire-and-brimstone talk. He jumped up suddenly and started yelling in a booming voice. It was in Swahili and I didn't understand much of it, but there was no mistaking the fierceness of the tone. He went around the room laying hands on people's heads and yelling to the ceiling, I assume to ask assistance to "drive out the devil." The parishioners started swaying and moaning. Lightness smiled and gave me a knowing look as I got up and backed into a corner to hide. Thankfully the pastor walked past me with no comment, because I didn't know what I would do if he laid his hands on me.

After he did his rounds on the adults, he called the children up to the front of the room for a special blessing, which, thankfully, was given in a gentler tone. Then he turned and went out the same door he had entered. The parishioners spoke quietly among themselves as a bowl was passed around to collect offerings.

The sun was going down when we walked back to the house. "So, what did you think of our meeting?" asked Lightness.

I admitted to her that it had somewhat unnerved me. "It is just so different from the church services I have been to before. I did go to a similar Pentecostal meeting in the South of our country once, and they did the same moaning, swaying, and laying of hands. It unnerved me then, also."

"We have many churches here," she laughed. "Maybe someday you will see a witch doctor. But tomorrow I will take you to my regular Lutheran church, and I think you will be comfortable there. But look who is here!" she suddenly said, eyeing the motorcycle in the yard as we walked up to her house.

It was obvious that Lightness was happy to see that her eldest son, Yohannes, had shown up for dinner. He was a handsome young man and cut a serious figure, despite the leather jacket over his professional attire. He was home on semester break from his job as a secondary school teacher in the Kilimanjaro region. Over dinner, we discussed local politics and the education system.

"I want to go back to school but it's difficult," he said. "I want to become a politician so I can help my country. I have a scholarship to a University in Sweden but they haven't accepted my visa application. They only take so many

Africans. All I can do is wait and apply again next year if I can't get the visa in time." I admired his ambition and wished him well.

After dinner, Lightness would not accept my help in cleaning up, so I sat in the living room with Yohannes and the continuous blare of a television set, which seemed permanently tuned to a Nigerian station with non-stop religious services, mostly in English. Most of the people wore what I would call choir robes. Occasionally there were men in traditional African dress, made out of reeds or colorful cloth, who were "saved." Parts of the services were subdued, but there was also a lot of singing, dancing, and over-the-top showmanship.

Yohannes, Lightness and I watched and talked intermittently. I didn't want to be rude, but I was getting sleepy and it was a struggle not to yawn. Thankfully, Yohannes excused himself first and Lightness and I followed soon after. I had been a little concerned about where I would sleep, but I was led to a comfortable Western-style bedroom and bath that would have been unremarkable in America. In the compound, I shared a bed with Katie, so it was nice to have a whole room to myself again.

The next day, as promised, we walked to the Lutheran church. I took my small overnight bag with me, since it was in the same direction as the compound. The church was housed in a large, airy, modern building with a lot of stone and glass. Yohannes immediately excused himself to go greet old friends. Lightness introduced me to some people before we sat and enjoyed a nice service with a band and youth singing groups to provide entertainment. The sermon was mostly in English, and the tone was vastly different from what I had experienced the night before.

"Most of the people in my country are Christian, but there

were different kinds of missionaries sent here," Lightness explained. "Originally people went to the missionaries for food, clothing, and education, but now I think we are more Christian than you, from what I have seen on television."

The Christianity I saw in Tanzania seemed very dogmatic, but the people seemed to internalize the values into their everyday lives. I definitely heard a lot of "Praise the Lord!" and "God be willing" in conversations. For many in the United States, it is just a social thing to do on Sundays. I was raised in the Lutheran church but now considered myself more of a seeker than a Christian. Some of the alternatives seemed to have much better views of the world and how we can survive and thrive together on this planet.

I hated that Christianity seemed to have been forced on the African people by their subjugators, but appreciated that they had put their own stamp on it and that it was a major binding force in communities. "What religion are you?" was often one of the first things I was asked when I met native Africans.

After church, we walked to the hospital where Lightness worked.

"I want to introduce my sister from America," she said again and again as we wandered through the one-story building, greeting people. In the surgical suite, I saw a table with some instruments laid out on a blue towel.

"We don't have a sterilizer so we just wash the instruments in hot, soapy water," Lightness explained. "It's not ideal but, God willing, it will be enough."

We came to a large room with windows along two sides and rows of metal beds beneath the windows. This was the women's ward, and women in blue cotton gowns with colorful headwraps sat on the beds, chatting with their neighbors and visitors. I only saw one intravenous line, and was told the woman was being prepared for a C-section. Patients with infectious diseases like AIDS and tuberculosis were not separated from the others.

"There's just not room," Lightness explained. "Children are taught in primary school to be careful of blood and to cough into their elbows instead of their hands. It has helped, but there are still too many that get sick."

I nodded, aware that I still had the habit of coughing into my hand instead of my arm. I washed my hands a lot, but I wished that behavior had been ingrained in me when I was a child. I never even noticed it until I was an adult in another country, *after* I had been to nursing school. It just wasn't a thing when I was in school. If we didn't have Kleenex, we coughed into our hands. It's a hard habit to break, so I was glad to see the kids were being taught to cough more hygienically.

The nursery was a single windowless room off to one side. The concrete walls made it seem cold and it was bare except for one metal crib and a portable heater. A shelf held suction bulbs, small syringes, and infant formula. There were no special lights to treat newborn jaundice. I knew they had a high infant mortality rate in Tanzania, and I wondered if the patient mortality rate was high as well.

"Where are the twins you delivered yesterday?" I asked Lightness.

Her wide smile matched her name. "They were in excellent shape and went home this morning."

"Thank you so much for sharing your home, your church, and your hospital with me," I said, as she walked me the rest of the way back to the compound. "It means a lot to me to see how medical care is done in your country."

"I like to meet other medical workers and compare what is good and bad here. There is always room to improve." She

41

grinned as she added, "I hope you find what you're looking for."

I wasn't sure what she meant, but I smiled and gave her a goodbye hug. I thought about what she said as I walked on. What was I looking for? I had come to Africa to get some distance from my normal life, which the end of employment and marriage had changed drastically.

There was no going back, but what did forward look like? I wasn't sure, but I wanted to follow this road and see where it led. Staying home and finding a new job would have been the easy way. Most of my life had been easy, and it felt pretty mediocre. I was determined that finding the new normal would be an adventure.

At the end of the two weeks, our bus driver showed up again and drove us back to Dar es Salaam. We were tired from being immersed in a vastly different culture. Most people were scheduled to leave for their permanent assignments the next day. Some were taking private cars or flying, depending on what their sponsor paid for.

"It will take two days for me to get to my assignment on the bus," complained Rachel, "but I'm excited to finally get to my new home."

My work site was in Ngara, 650 miles across the country and about twenty-two hours' driving time. I would be living with Anna, a 25-year-old volunteer from New York whom I had met but hadn't spent much time with.

"I'm so glad our sponsor arranged for his driver to take us in his car," she said. "A bus would probably take twice as long and be twice as uncomfortable."

"Yes," I agreed. "And cause twice the worry about our belongings getting there unmolested."

"Not to mention ourselves," she laughed.

4

HOME, FINALLY

...people knew nothing of things they might have had. A Frigidaire? A washer/dryer combination? Really, they'd sooner imagine a tree that would pull up its feet and go bake bread. It didn't occur to them to feel sorry for themselves.

— BARBARA KINGSOLVER, *THE POISONWOOD BIBLE*

---

*W*hen I decided to spend a year volunteering in Africa, I envisioned living in a jungle environment like in the *Tarzan* movies, with lots of vines, rivers, and jungle-covered hills. I knew this was a fantasy and that most of the movies were filmed in Florida. I had been to Africa when I was young and knew that a lot of it was desert and grassland. I had grown up with *Tarzan*, though, and it was still my dream to go to Africa, meet the challenges there, and somehow come home triumphant.

Triumphant over what, I'm not sure. Historically, it seems to be the white man's folly that he can go somewhere foreign, "improve" it, and make it more like where he came from. Roads, trains, modern farms, and air conditioning can improve a place. But I have learned that native cultures have much to offer and are often more suited to the place they inhabit because they have evolved to fit it.

I didn't go to Africa with the idea that I would change the continent, or even the community I lived in. I think my journey was more about conquering myself and my fears, and proving that I had the strength and ability to manage in a totally different culture. I also wanted to influence some of my students, especially the girls, by showing them that their dreams could be bigger than the village they lived in. Tanzania has a patriarchal society, and violence against women is common. Most of the farming is done by women, leaving men comparatively more time for leisure and social activities. More women are pursuing higher education and finding their voices, however, and over a third of the national parliamentary seats are now held by women.

I was a little disappointed to find myself assigned to a farming community on the other side of the country. Its position near the Rwandan border had made Ngara an ideal spot for U.N. headquarters and refugee camps during the Genocide in Rwanda in the mid-1990s, when over a million people lost their lives in a political frenzy. I pictured flat land and chaos, which didn't fit in with my jungle fantasy.

Ashley tried to reassure me. "It's a great place with lots of amenities like restaurants and ATMs. And you'll only have to walk a mile to school."

Anna, a petite, green-eyed redhead with a mass of auburn curls that flowed to her waist, was to be my partner at our assigned community of Ngara. We were fortunate that our sponsor, the local Member of Parliament, dispatched his Toyota Land Runner to transport us. We made the trip in sixteen hours of driving time instead of the several days it would have taken on a bus.

Gigi, the lanky six-foot-tall African driver, was polite but seemed to be always laughing at us. "I would have just pulled off the side of the road to rest," he told me, as we checked into a hotel along the way for an overnight rest. "You *mzungus* (foreigners) are spoiled, so you need a bed and hot food."

I didn't contradict him. A bed and hot food were very welcome. We had already driven twelve hours across flat, barren land that reminded me more of the Mojave Desert than the lush jungle I pictured when I thought of Africa. The only relief in the landscape were occasional baobabs, barrel-like trees with mushroom-shaped tops that looked like they belonged less to earth than to some fantasy world in a galaxy far away. The road was paved, but we often had to take bumpy detours on dirt roads due to "road work" and saw several work crews of sweaty Africans being yelled at by Chinese overseers in trucks. Villages were few and far between, but all had a series of often unmarked speed bumps leading up to them, so you had to pass through them slowly.

On the road again the next day, my phone beeped as we were riding through a particularly desolate stretch with a few scattered shacks but no people in sight. The car didn't have air conditioning and the stream of dust blowing in the open windows along with the hot, dry air did not help our comfort. My skin felt caked in dirt and my throat clogged in dust. There was no conversation, as it seemed more prudent to keep our mouths closed. I dug my phone out of my pocket, brushing off dirt as I held it to my ear.

"I just wanted to check on you," Ashley said, her bubbly

personality at odds with our distress. "You're so lucky to be able to cross the country. Isn't the scenery stunning?"

"Well, you could say that," I replied, scrunching down in my seat and adjusting the scarf across my face so I could talk without getting a mouthful of grit. We hit a bump and a cloud of dust covered the windshield.

"Enjoy your trip. I'll come visit in a couple of weeks," Ashley promised before hanging up.

Finally we started up the hills that led to the border region. There was more vegetation but I was a little disappointed because it looked like my native Southern California in the dry season, very unlike my expectations for the place.

"I've come so far and it's like I never left home," I thought to myself.

Of course, our housing wasn't ready yet. TIA. Gigi settled us in at a Catholic retreat outside of town, told us to "Just wait," and quickly departed. Our room was pretty barren, with unfinished wood plank floors and wide cracks in the wood plank walls that let the hot outside air in. The two single beds had highly-patched cotton bedspreads. A dresser with a pitcher of water took up one corner. Luckily, we had some bottled water with us so we didn't have to take a chance on drinking it.

Anna and I sat on our beds and looked at each other. "Now what?" we asked ourselves. Exhausted from the heat and the long trip, Anna punched at her pillow and laid down. "When in doubt, take a nap!" she exclaimed. After reading for a short while, I drifted off to sleep as well.

A few hours later, loud knocking on the door awakened us. Anna groggily dragged herself off of the bed and opened the door. A tall, stout, middle-aged black woman in a flowing, floor length pastel dress and a large turban of the same fabric stood there with a huge grin on her face. I

46

stood up to greet the only person we had seen since our arrival.

"I'm Mama Caritas. I'm the head of the local school district and am happy to welcome you to Ngara," she said, emphasizing the "N" before following with "gahrah." The feeling of being a cast-off orphan left me as Mama Caritas took us under her wing and told us she would show us our schools and then take us to dinner.

"Unfortunately, you will have to stay here for a few days until your house is ready."

"We get our own house?" I said, not sure if that was good or bad. Ashley had told us that most teachers shared communal housing on school property or nearby. Maybe the other teachers had protested when informed they would have *mzungus* living among them.

"Yes, you will see," she replied vaguely. I wondered if there really was a house or they simply didn't know where to put us.

She led us out to her car, an older model Ford. She apparently had an important position because she had her own driver. We drove through the town of Ngara, which consisted of one asphalt road with several dirt roads leading off it to clusters of ramshackle one- and two-story buildings with faded whitewash exteriors and rusty tin roofs.

After a few blocks, the town ended and we continued for several miles up a hill through some banana fields until we arrived at a flat open area. The few concrete buildings were positioned on the edge of a cliff overlooking a river several hundred feet below.

"This is Murgwanza Secondary School," Mama Caritas said. The school was only a few years old and I liked its location perched on a cliff top with dramatic views of Rwanda across the river. The classrooms were spacious and large windows let in a lot of light, even though there was no electricity. We met some of the staff, who seemed very welcoming. This was Anna's assigned school. I hoped mine would be as nice.

Mama Caritas piled us back into the car and we drove several miles to the other side of town. About a quarter of a mile up a dirt road we had to wait for someone to lift a long bar across the road. On top of the hill there was a cluster of buildings that made up Ngara Secondary School.

My school was older and larger than Anna's and had 850 students. The largest building was for administration and the teachers' lounge. Four one-story buildings divided into two classrooms each and a separate smaller building that housed a library surrounded a large open area with many boulders scattered around. Several students in their uniforms of turquoise sweaters and black pants or green mid-calf skirts lounged in groups among the rocks, apparently oblivious to us. Mama Caritas pointed out housing for teachers off to one side and down a hill. I wondered if this is where we would live.

"No, your house is not ready yet," Mama Caritas declared, offering no more information.

The administration building was the only one that had electricity. The sole computer was locked away in an office and available only to the principal, vice principal and secretary. The teachers' lounge had several long tables with wooden chairs pulled up snugly beneath them. A small color TV blared out a news program. I couldn't imagine the small town had a television station so I wasn't sure of the origin of the news. It could have come from a thousand or more miles away, as far as I knew. Judging from what I had seen, I was fairly certain the car accidents in front of large multistory buildings did not happen anywhere nearby.

As we stood outside surveying the property, a big motorcycle revved up the hill and screeched to a stop. The giant-sized, black leather-clad driver lifted his leg over the motorcycle, pulling the silver helmet and mask off at the same time. As his arms came down, my first impression was of a very tall, handsome, young black man. I couldn't imagine who he could be, but he looked too old to be a student. His dramatic entrance reminded me more of a superhero.

"Hello, I'm Mr. Soharo, the principal," he said, grinning. "You must be the new volunteer."

I was a little taken aback because I was used to school principals who wore suits and ties and drove sedate sedans. We chatted for a few minutes until Mama Caritas directed us back to the car. The tour was over and she had to go back to work at her office.

∾

We stayed in our sauna-like room at the Catholic retreat for a few more days, the only air conditioning provided by the large cracks between the boards that made up the walls. Mama Caritas came every day to check on us, and every day we asked her when our house would be ready. "Soon," was always the answer, but any other questions on the subject were met with silence.

She introduced us to the canteen on the property, where we could mingle with the nuns and priests, who all seemed to have taken a vow of silence. After saying hello to the waitress, Anna and I would point to items on the limited menu written in chalk on the wall. It consisted of mainly bread, eggs, and potatoes but sometimes featured fish and chips.

We walked around the area a little to get some exercise, but we were far from town and there didn't seem to be anything of interest nearby except lots of trees with long broad leaves that sometimes shielded bananas or papayas. The fruits looked delicious, but we had no way to climb up to get them, and they never appeared on the menu.

On our third day at the compound, Mama Caritas and her driver took us to the small village of Rulenge, about twenty miles away, to visit two fellow volunteers, Laura and Kerry. They were staying at the house of our fellow sponsor, the same Member of Parliament who had lent us his car and driver for the journey there. He was away at the capital for a few months to take care of Parliamentary duties, so they had free run of the house. I was in awe as the keeper of the iron entrance gate let us into the courtyard and I saw the beautiful, modern, tile-roofed house and lush gardens. It had been less than a week since we had parted from Laura and Kerry, but my mind was jarred by the abnormality of suddenly seeing a white person besides Anna. I had no time to reflect on how strange that was as they ushered us into the house for a tour. Laura boasted about the solar power, marble bathroom, stove, refrigerator, television, and ceiling fans. There were four bedrooms, so they each had one to themselves.

"I haven't seen anything like this since I left home," I said. "We could be back in America… a nice part of America. He must be very rich."

Mama Caritas came in from outside, where she had been talking with the gardener/watchman. "The MP was born in this village," she explained. "His parents were relatively wealthy farmers, so he had the opportunity to pursue an advanced degree in the capital. After that, he made a lot of money in business before deciding to run for Parliament.

"My hope is that you can encourage some of your students to follow after him," she continued. "Most of the people around here are farmers, but the farms don't produce enough. The children get married and have more children and everyone is depending on the same plot of land to live. They need to be educated so they have more options. And they need to stay away from AIDS."

"Yes, we saw the big billboards in Dar from the Ministry of Education that said 'Make A's, not AIDS,'" I told her.

"We have a million and a half people with AIDS, and over a million orphans because of it," she said. "That's why we put it in the curriculum at every grade level."

We sat at the large Formica kitchen table while Laura and Kerry served us the last of the tea and biscuits they had bought in Dar es Salaam. Mama Caritas wanted to know why we had come to Africa. Laura was taking a year off before she started medical school and Kerry had graduated but wasn't sure what she wanted to do. Anna, my roommate, had been working and traveling on and off since she graduated from college several years before. She joined WorldTeach to get some overseas experience so she could work for an international aid agency.

Mama Caritas set down her tea and looked at me intently. "And why are you here, Mama?" Mama was apparently used as a sign of respect to address anyone "of a certain age."

It seemed trite to tell them my life was boring and I needed a challenge. The girls were on the other end of life, with a smorgasbord of choices and seemingly infinite time to experiment. With the luxury of time, a poor choice is never a mistake, just a learning experience. Youth provides the luxury to regroup and choose another door, one that may lead to more education, travel, new relationships, interesting jobs, marriage, and children. The young can close a door at any time and try the experiences again with different people in different places.

I remembered being on that side of life. It was hard to explain to them that I wanted some of that feeling again: the exhilaration of flinging open new doors when I was not sure what would be on the other side. There are not many bad doors in the United States if you have the money to fix your mistakes and you are able to avoid drugs, poor health, and energy-sapping relationships.

I hoped, at this stage of my life, to be able to make better choices. I did not want to squander my remaining years on a life with no purpose or "mistakes" that might never be overcome. I wanted to challenge myself, but I wanted a fall-back plan so I could make the best use of my remaining time.

One reason I chose one year with WorldTeach instead of the Peace Corps is that two and a half years seemed like too long to commit to any one thing, especially when I had limited control over the outcome. I had filled out a Peace Corps application when I was in my twenties and time was not a consideration, because I would still be a young adult when I got out. I chose a different door when I went into the Army to train to be a nurse, thinking I could travel overseas. Although a lot of people in my class were sent to Korea and Germany, the government, in their infinite wisdom, stationed me in my home state of California.

I had often wondered what my life would have been like if I had stuck with my original plan and joined the Peace Corps. I still wanted the experience of going to a foreign place, putting myself out there, and trying to make a difference. Just traveling for a few weeks once a year no longer seemed enough. I was long past thinking I could save the world, but I thought I might at least plant some seeds, even if I wasn't around long enough to see them take root.

I looked up to see everyone's eyes on me, so I told the simple truth. "I wanted to come to Africa to teach."

They all nodded because wasn't that why all of the volunteers were here? But the truth is never simple. Over time, I got to know the stories of overbearing parents or boyfriends, of escaping a town they had lived in all their lives, of angst about starting or staying in a profession, or just "finding out who I am."

I guess the latter also applied to me, because even at my age, I felt there were pieces of me still to be discovered. Or rediscovered. It felt like this experience might be the jump-start to a new me and a new life, something, if not bigger and better, more intimate and satisfying.

∼

One day, Mama Caritas showed up after breakfast. "I have a house for you," she declared, "but it is only temporary."

Anna and I were glad to get away from the Catholic retreat and hoped we could begin preparing our own food. We ascribed our increasingly sluggish feeling to a high carbohydrate diet and not enough exercise.

The car followed the paved highway for a few miles before turning up a dirt road through a banana plantation. We stopped at a rusty gate that had the tall metal letters "UNHCR" embedded, which I later found out stood for "United Nations High Commission for Refugees." The compound, known as Afriline, had been built during the Rwandan civil war in the 1990s, when tribal resentments flared into the Genocide that killed over a million people, or one sixth of that country's population. Refugee camps were set up around the town, but killers snuck across the border and murdered people in the camps.

"You Americans talk about how shocked you were when so many people died on 9/11, but around here it was like having a 9/11 every day for months," Mama Caritas declared. "We had refugee children in the schools, and the

53

teachers were afraid they would get killed trying to protect them."

Ngara sits on the Tanzanian side of the river that separates the two countries. At the time of the Genocide, it was considered a prime location for refugee camps and the United Nations headquarters that oversaw them. The old U.N. office building in town now housed the Department of Education, including the office of Mama Caritas.

Afriline contained the living quarters of the long-gone peacekeepers and was now inhabited by various mid-level government employees and occasional government visitors. The cinder block houses had metal roofs loosely covered in thatch. We wandered past several clusters of them and the central canteen building, which housed a neighborhood club/restaurant, now eerily quiet. There was even a building with a squash court. All of it was surrounded by an eight-foot-tall chain link fence with barbed wire running along the top. I could see cows grazing on the other side of the fence. All of the U.N. employees must have brought plants from their home countries, because the compound was lush with flowers and trees that I doubted were indigenous to Africa, such as eucalyptus, roses, and Japanese maples.

According to Mama Caritas, the house the school district was providing for us was temporarily occupied by some ministry officials. They were there to investigate the killing of six Rwandan shepherds, who had reportedly wandered over to Tanzania looking for better grazing land. It would be difficult to cross the border by accident, because the signs on the bridge over the river that divided the two countries were impossible to ignore, including pictures and words in three languages. The prevailing theory was that they had come over to do mischief, got caught in the act, and were killed by locals protecting their property. These suppositions were apparently enough to file a report and close the case, because they vacated our house two days later.

In the meantime, we stayed in a temporary house in the same compound that had a stunning view from the porch that ran along the whole back side of the house and overlooked the river valley. I was loathe to leave it, even though the lights did not work and we were limited to candles and flash-lights. Also, there was no hot water, mosquito nets, or any place to cook.

It still felt like an improvement over the Catholic retreat because we had solid concrete block walls instead of peeling wood. The only thing that really unsettled us were the trucks full of armed soldiers that protected the visiting Ministry offi-cials around the clock.

When we finally got the key and opened the door to our new house two days later, we found the bathroom, living room, and bedrooms flooded with water. We were told it had been cleaned, and I thought the previous tenants or the maid must have left a faucet on. Mama Caritas sent plumbers from town, but they couldn't find the source of any water leak.

They cleaned up the mess and made a list of supplies they would need to redo the plumbing and meet our requests for hot water and good water pressure. The water was running, but the water heater and shower would have to wait. They showed us where rodents had apparently chewed up the wire attached to the old water heater.

Mama Caritas took their list, along with our request for mosquito nets and something to cook on, which Ashley had told us was in our contract with the Ministry of Education. There was a space and outlet for an oven, but she told us our request for a refrigerator and washing machine were not an option. Her continual smile seemed to be failing somewhat that day.

I went to inspect my new bedroom and was surprised to see that a king-sized bed took up almost the whole room.

"Africans are used to sharing," Mama Caritas explained. "Your room would fit a whole family, so you are lucky to each have your own room."

I inspected the generous built-in closet before I turned back to her and startled.

"Watch out!" I screamed, as I backed up into the closet door. "What are those huge things on the wall?"

Mama Caritas turned around and calmly examined three fist-sized hairy black spiders. She held her hand up and they moved six feet away in the blink of an eye.

"Don't be afraid. They like dark, unoccupied houses. They will probably go away once you are living here," she said.

"Are they poisonous?" I asked, holding my place by the closet door, afraid to get close to the other wall.

"Yes, but they will never bite you. They like insects and small rodents," she smiled.

I wasn't sure if that was a joke, but I was determined to sleep with the light on that night.

Mama Caritas took us to the market in town, which consisted of individual stalls in several huge, old United Nations canvas tents. She bought us a kerosene stove, which looked to me like a backpacking stove, as a temporary measure. The toothless old women who managed the stalls had beautiful fruits and vegetables. We purchased some food and basic cooking supplies, like pots, dishes, and eating utensils, which set us back over $100.

After Mama Caritas dropped us off at our new home, we gamely tried to cook dinner, but were frustrated that it took an hour to get the water boiling and another hour to cook some potatoes. We had to use the stove on the open porch due to the toxic black smoke it produced. We gave up on cooking anything else that night and mixed the potatoes with raw tomatoes and onions to make a salad.

On subsequent days we ate a lot of peanut butter and bananas. It was a forty-minute walk to the market in town, and we were limited to what we could carry back to our house. Luckily, we were able to buy plastic bottles of drinking water at the Afriline restaurant and only had to carry them a short distance up the road. The environmentalist in me cringed at the lack of any plastic recycling in the whole country. We were actually told to *burn* the bottles. The resulting nasty fumes made me sure I was polluting the air enough to kill some babies.

Ashley had assured us that there was an ATM in town, so we hadn't loaded up with cash before we left Dar es Salaam. We felt that being *mzungus* made us targets for robbery and hadn't wanted to carry a lot of cash on the overland trip. Our teaching stipends wouldn't start for another three weeks. It was a shock to discover that the sole bank in town did not accept credit cards and only accepted Tanzanian ATM cards. After spending most of our cash on supplies, we were unexpectedly broke. We called Mama Caritas for help and she took us to meet the bank manager, a short, bald man who exchanged some of our dwindling supply of American dollars for us as a favor to her.

"I can only do this one time," he said, sounding like he was scolding us for being stupid enough to come to town with no money. "There is an ATM in Mwanza. It's only about ten hours on the bus."

We looked at Mama Caritas and Anna whined, "But we have to go to school and the banks won't be open on the weekend!"

I was sure Mama's eyes were mentally raised to the

ceiling as she patiently said, "I will make sure you get a Thursday off." Since we only worked Monday through Thursday, that would give us plenty of time to go and come back. The thought of sitting ten hours on a bus was not appealing, though.

Adding to our distress, Mama Caritas told us that the plumber, mosquito nets, and a "proper" stove would have to wait until the new Ministry of Education budget was passed, "maybe next week."

I groaned as I thought of another week of feeling like I was sleeping in a shroud, tugging the sheets over my head as I listened to the whine of mosquitoes at night. It was strange to be in actual discomfort and not to be able to pull out a credit card or get money to fix the problem.

Gigi was right. Americans are spoiled.

5

SCHOOL DAZE

It's good to do uncomfortable things. It's weight training for life.

— ANNE LAMOTT, *PLAN B: FURTHER THOUGHTS ON FAITH*

---

*T*he second night in our new house, a loud noise jolted me awake and the vibrations passed through my body as my eyes opened suddenly to darkness. No, more than darkness; a thick inky blackness with no hint of light anywhere. My mind skittered, latching on to the fact that this was my first day of school and I couldn't just roll over and go back to sleep.

My hand reached out blindly to stop the buzz of the alarm clock. I felt my arm connect with something and heard a crash on the floor, along with what sounded like some papers and probably the flashlight I had put by my bed in case of electrical failure. I sat up on the side of the bed and, still groggy, reached forward for the opposite wall so I could feel my way along it to the light switch. I misjudged the distance, because my hand just kept on going.

Flailing in a sea of blackness, I lost perception of right and left, up and down. Everything slowed down as I swam in the inky currents. My forehead was the first thing to concede to gravity as I hit the concrete floor. I yelled, but heard no answer from my housemate, who was apparently enjoying the luxury of sleeping in, since her school didn't start until the next day. Lucky her.

I crawled over to the wall, wanting to make contact before I tried to rise. I thought of the large fuzzy spiders that seemed to like the walls and the dark and prayed my hand didn't make contact with one. Thankfully my sliding fingers only found the light switch. I gave it a few up and down tugs with no response, dashing my hopes that the power was not really out. My hands slid back along the wall to the window and pulled the curtain aside. No sign of the floodlights that should be streaming over the compound. No ambient light from stars or neon signs. I fleetingly thought of a terrorist attack, but everything was too quiet. It felt like the blackness extended indefinitely, and I was alone on a sea of nothingness.

I crouched down into the void, being careful to keep one hand anchored on the wall while feeling around the floor for the lost flashlight. Aside from the shock of the fall, I had been pretty calm up to now but became increasingly anxious as my searching hand did not find my only possible source of light on the floor or on the bedside chair that served as my nightstand.

My anxiety hadn't quite reached panic level when I remembered that I had put the flashlight in my backpack the night before, in preparation for my first day of school. I felt my way around the king-sized bed. The day before, I had complained about it taking up most of the room, but now I was thankful that its size allowed me to use one side as a table, making it easy to find the backpack and the clothes I had laid out. Soon a small stream of light penetrated the darkness and I was able to dress and turn my mind to the not-yet-routine tasks of getting ready for school.

"I'm almost sixty years old! I feel like I'm back in high school!" I grumbled, as I got dressed and lamented my interrupted sleep.

I opened the bedroom door, my small light directed ahead of me, and stepped forward. Immediately my bare foot was awash in cold and wet. I inhaled quickly in surprise and aimed my light down. Not just a puddle; the whole floor was covered in water. I exhaled in dismay and sloshed over to the kitchen sink. The water wasn't running or even dripping. I opened the doors underneath the sink to check for drips there. The pipes were glistening with wetness. I put the flashlight in my mouth so I could use both hands to tighten the connection. The whole thing fell apart in my hands and water gushed out.

Now I panicked. I reflexively opened my mouth and the forgotten flashlight fell out. My emotions tumbled from horror to relief as I was able to catch it before it hit the water. Almost immediately, I was back to horror as I slid on the wet floor and almost went down while running toward the water shutoff valve in the bathroom.

"Thank goodness they showed us where it was before they left yesterday," I muttered. "Two plumbers couldn't find the problem, but I sure did. TIA." This is Africa.

Water was everywhere on the floor, but no longer in the pipes. The toilet had enough water in the tank for one flush. I thought of the surprise Anna would find when she woke up. At least she didn't have to worry about school that day.

I used bottled water to clean my teeth, slapped on some deodorant and brushed my hair. There was no time to wait for the charcoal stove to boil water for coffee. I grabbed a bottle of water and a granola bar to eat on the way. I raised my hand to my forehead and felt the bump rising there.

Sighing, I grabbed a towel and went out to the porch to dry my feet and put on my shoes. Finally, I took out my cell phone and left a text for Anna: "Have a great day off. Call the plumber for leak below kitchen sink."

I stepped off the porch, thinking what a good impression I would make on my first day of school, battered and late. Sadly, my morning battle was not over. Because of the darkness, I didn't notice the thick fog until I stepped off the porch. No wonder the air felt thick and I couldn't see any stars. I pointed my meager light ahead of me on the dirt road, jumping over a few huge ruts until I came to the guard station. I couldn't see anyone around so I knocked on the door of the small wooden hut next to the gate.

"*Habari!*" I called out as I knocked. "Good morning!"

I stepped back as a yawning hulk came out of the dark hut, making no eye contact as he wordlessly unlocked and opened the gate for me.

"*Asante sana.* Thank you very much," I said as I walked out of the compound. I heard him grunt as he closed and locked the gate. I looked behind me, but the gate and the guard had been swallowed up by the dark fog.

What was normally a pleasant twenty-minute walk through banana fields to the main road became a perilous, spooky trek down the rutted dirt road, dodging rocks and holes. The bright headlights of the two cars that passed me gave a few moments of relief from the near absolute darkness.

Suddenly, a shadow carrying a machete walked out of a

grove of tall banana trees right in front of me. Taken aback, I stopped and stared at a wrinkled face surrounded by long, straggly gray hair and at the foot-long blade the ghost woman raised to her chest. I was frozen in terror as I waited for her to raise it further above her head and yell, "Die, *mzungu*!"

"*Shikamo*," she said, as she bowed her head slightly and kept walking.

My terror abated as I recognized the greeting of respect.

"*Marahaba*," I answered, hoping it was the correct response. I turned to watch her go but she had already disappeared into the fog.

By the time I got to the paved main road, dawn had lightened the sky enough that I could turn off my flashlight. The all-encompassing fog was dissipating into swirling mists. I trudged onward, my head aching from stress, lack of coffee, and the not inconsiderable goose egg on my forehead.

The number of cars increased as I passed the still-sleeping town and shadowy figures passed me in the fog. After almost an hour of walking, I reached the sign that marked the dirt road leading up to Ngara Secondary School. I checked my cell phone and noted that I was going to be fifteen minutes late. There was no message from Anna, so hopefully she would get a good sleep before she had to deal with the plumbing and electricity.

"First days of school suck!" I said loudly. My headache increased as I walked up the hill to the school, feeling like a truant schoolgirl. "This is a terrible way to start, but it can't get any worse," I reassured myself, mentally crossing my fingers.

I trudged up the hill and found hundreds of students, identifiable by their turquoise sweaters, black pants, and green skirts, gathered in the central area surrounded by the numerous buildings that made up the school. The principal and a group of teachers stood on a rise, slightly above the gathering.

"Oh, good!" I thought to myself. "Maybe nobody will notice I'm late."

I should have remembered that eagle-eyed principals see all.

"Here is our new volunteer teacher. Come up here and I will introduce you," he said loudly.

All eyes were upon me as I slowly made my way through the crowd to the top of the rise. I fleetingly wondered if I'd put my shirt on right side out and the buttons in the right holes as I dressed in the dark. I felt the side of my head and the goose egg that seemed to have doubled in size since the last time I checked.

"Namaste," I said, dipping my head before realizing that was for another time and another country. "Good Morning!" I cried, increasing my volume to in hopes of covering my mistake.

"Good morning, teacher!" the students responded loudly. "Oh, well trained," I thought to myself as I struggled for something else to say.

"I have come from the United States to be with you and teach you. I hope you can learn from me, and I hope I will learn from you. I'm so happy to be here." I glanced aside and noticed the Principal beaming. Maybe I hadn't flubbed this after all.

One last big smile and a wave for the students and I stepped aside. The side of my foot hit a rock and I was suddenly flailing again. That seemed to be my theme for the day. Strong arms caught me and set me on my feet. I was so flustered, I didn't even notice who they belonged to, just shut my eyes and wished the day over.

"Yes," I reaffirmed to myself. "First days of school suck!"

64

I quickly discovered that the first week of school was "environmental week," when students clean the school in preparation for the semester ahead. There was no paid custodial staff, so students were responsible for cleaning, gardening, and bringing water in buckets (usually carried on their heads!) from the river, which was about a quarter of a mile away.

"You really don't need to come this week, since you're new and you don't speak Swahili," the Principal said. "A lot of the students won't understand your directions. Come back on Monday."

"Now he tells me," I mentally fumed, trying to keep my smile from slipping, as I thought of all the trials and tribulations I had suffered to get there that morning in the pitch dark.

The coming days would have been a good time to take our needed trip to Mwanza to get some cash, except Anna's principal decided they needed her at school. That left me home all week waiting for the plumber and electrician to show up. The latter promptly fixed the electrical problem by getting our landlord to put money in the meter.

The plumber was more elusive, and missed three appointments in a row before showing up. I had put the PVC pipes back together with twist ties but needed him to attach them more permanently. He looked at my makeshift repair and blamed the whole problem on me, ignoring the fact that he had inspected the house the week before and told us he couldn't find anything to explain the occasional floods.

"You caused the problem so you need to pay me some money," he said slyly, after completing a more permanent repair.

"No, you didn't find the problem. Thank you for fixing it.

The school board has agreed to pay you, so you'll have to ask them for your money," I said firmly.

"*Mzungus*," he grunted, shaking his head as he shuffled out the door.

~

I felt ready for my real first day at school the next week. A few nights of good sleep and free time to study Swahili made me feel much more prepared. After buying some plastic tubs and stringing nylon rope across our patio, we were able to wash our growing pile of dirty clothes. The electricity hadn't failed all week and we finally had a working shower, if not hot running water. Rodents had chewed up the wires leading to the water heater and that still needed to be fixed.

Mama Caritas told us what became her usual line: "It's not in the budget this month."

We were eating better, having found a good supply of fresh fruits and vegetables, a vendor at the bottom of the hill who made fresh, hot chapatis to order, and a bakery in town that made fresh bread twice a week. Organization and a few wall decorations made our place feel more homey. Things were looking up. It's strange how little things like a piece of fruit or fresh bread were causes for major excitement, but we were living in a different world.

For my "homework" during environmental week, I was given a large 14-by-20 inch blank piece of paper and told to put my plan for the semester on the single page, with a row for each week of each month, so that the school administration had a rough idea of what I was teaching on any one day. My only guidance was a ten-page pamphlet of guidelines for teaching Form 1 English from the Tanzanian Ministry of Education (the school's only copy, so I had to return it on

Monday) and the Principal telling me that I had to include everything in it in my plan. Other than that, it was up to me to decide when and how to teach it. There were no textbooks or teaching aids.

The classrooms had "blackboards" in the front of each room, which consisted of black paint on the concrete walls. I was given one pack of "dustless" chalk and told I could get three pieces at a time from the office whenever I needed more. That proved to be quite often, since the pitted concrete ate up the chalk at an alarming rate, getting white chalk dust all over my hands and clothes. The teacher's desk and podium, positioned in front of the blackboards, were also covered with a layer of chalk dust.

My school schedule called for me to teach four streams of Form 1 English. Each "stream" consisted of about fifty students, who met with me for eighty-minute classes three times a week. Four classes repeated three times during the week might not sound like much, but my lessons were pretty much from scratch and required a lot of preparation, especially thinking of ways to keep so many students engaged for an hour and twenty minutes at a time.

The lone Monday morning class gave me a chance to experiment before duplicating or tweaking the material for the other streams that afternoon and on Tuesday. By Wednesday, I usually had a better idea of students' command of the material and went on from there. Sometimes, I realized I needed to teach primary material before I could even get to the scheduled subject. Other times, the students surprised me by already having a command of what I was trying to teach. One stream eventually ended up a week behind due to the need for remedial teaching, which created havoc with my schedule.

The better schooled "city kids" tended to sit near the front and sides of the classrooms, and the older, less knowledge-able "farmer kids" congregated in the back. Kevin, my youngest student, was ten years old and sat front and center, always dressed in an immaculate uniform, and actually ahead of most of the others because he had gone to a private primary school. Joshua, my oldest student, was nineteen years old and trying to make up for time lost when he dropped out of school to take care of the family farm after his father died of AIDS. He was earnest but seemed to have forgotten most of what he had learned when he was younger. He and many others needed individual attention that was hard to give when I had two hundred students to shepherd through the semester.

All of the student streams had their own "home" class-room in one of the three classroom buildings. I was used to a system where the students rotated to the teacher, but it was the opposite here. The students stayed in the same seat in the same classroom all semester, and the teachers rotated to them, following each stream's schedule. Most of the permanent teachers seemed to have their own desks in their department offices. I was told the first day that I would get a key to the Language Arts office but somehow never did, despite numerous requests. It was always "being made."

If I needed to get something from the office, I had to hunt down one of the permanent teachers and borrow a key. This didn't happen often, but not having a desk in a quiet office made it difficult to do individual tutoring. I tried to use the teachers' lounge and the library a couple of times, but was counseled against it. I tried sitting on a rock in the yard with individual students, but there were so many distractions from other students that I gave up after a few weeks.

I wasn't the only "homeless" teacher. There were several temporary teachers that had just finished high school and were waiting for acceptance to university. They were quite young themselves and I was told it only worked because they excelled in their subjects and came from different schools and districts. They were able to command a level of respect as teachers from their first day because nobody knew for sure how old they were.

"The government realized they needed a lot more schools because the youth population was exploding," Mama Caritas explained to Anna and me. "They went on a building binge, but soon realized they were short 8,000 teachers to staff the new schools. The Universities ramped up to turn out new teachers, but it's going to take a while to fill the gap."

"Is that why we're here?" Anna asked.

"I hire teachers where I can find them," answered Mama Caritas, looking skyward as if asking God to send her some more. "Some of the primary school teachers have only finished sixth grade. Primary school is taught in Swahili, and they do fine. The problem comes when the students enter secondary school, because it's taught in English. The students are supposed to learn English at each level of primary school, but very few of the teachers are fluent enough to teach it. That's why we need you."

That made me wonder if any of my students would be able to understand me. I had taught a refresher course to high school English teachers from South America the summer before, and their accents were so thick they couldn't even understand each other most of the time. I can't imagine what their students sounded like.

English and Swahili were official languages of Tanzania. I was told most of my students would be the children of farmers and mostly spoke the local tribal language in their homes. Everyone spoke at least some Swahili, which was the most common bridge language between the tribes. Secondary school was taught in English, which was a huge challenge to many students.

"Just speak slowly and write everything down so they can copy it," Mama Caritas advised. "A lot of the students aren't fluent, but they help each other. They know school is a path to a better life. They also know that if they don't learn English, they will never pass the Secondary School exams," she said, looking at me pointedly. It felt like the burden was on me for the students to succeed, since I was teaching first-year English.

"Mama Caritas, you're telling me that if I can't teach my students enough English to pass their exams, in whatever subject, they'll all fail and drop out."

"Just do your best," she smiled.

I made sure to arrive at school fifteen minutes early on Monday, my first day of teaching. The administrative secretary showed up about ten minutes later, but I didn't see the Principal for another half hour. He settled in and then took me to meet Melchior, the head of the Language Arts Department. He was a handsome man of medium height and dwarfed by the larger-than-life Principal, who left after a quick introduction.

"Good morning, Mrs. Morrison," he said, gazing at me calmly. He had a voice and manner that probably commanded a classroom without raising his voice, being preachy or an easy mark for mischief. I immediately felt that I could probably learn from him.

"Please don't call me that," I said, wanting to distance myself from the past and create a confident new persona. "Call me Mary."

"The students have to address you with respect," he replied. "But Mama Mary will work."

And, Mama Mary was born.

6

NGARA SECONDARY SCHOOL

Education is not a way of escaping poverty, it is a way of fighting it.

— JULIUS NYERERE

---

*B*y the time Melchior took me to my first class, it was almost over. It seemed the students were used to absent teachers, because they sat silently studying their notebooks. Each student was required to bring a small lined notebook with at least twenty-four pages, similar to what I would call an exam or spelling book, for taking notes. The notebooks appeared to be partially used up already, not all with English, as I saw a lot of math problems as I passed the nearest desks.

Melchior and I stood at the front of the class and he called out, "Good morning class!"

"Good morning, Teacher!" they responded loudly, standing up beside their chairs.

"I want to introduce you to your new teacher, Mama Mary."

"Good morning, Mama Mary!" they yelled, smiling for the most part. The white teeth stood out from their dark faces.

"Thank you!" I responded. "I look forward to meeting all of you and being your teacher." I looked around at the class. They stood tall and weren't slouching, which was a good sign. For the first time, I noticed that all their heads had been shaved. The only heads I couldn't see were those of the Muslim girls. I couldn't see through their white head scarves, but I assumed their heads were shaved as well.

Melchior told the class to return to what they were studying. After we walked outside, I asked about the head shaving.

"We used to have a problem with lice, especially with the girls and their complicated braids. We solved that," he said smugly.

I winced as I thought of what the girls had given up to go to school. Beauty shops with pictures of women in elaborate hairstyles were painted larger than life on outside walls all over the place.

"Everywhere I have been in Tanzania, I see women with beautiful, intricate braids," I said. "For a teenage girl aspiring to be a woman, that must be a huge sacrifice."

"They have to do it if they want to go to school," he replied unsympathetically. I later met his wife, a Swahili teacher at the school, who sported a very elaborate braided hairstyle. I doubted if she would have responded the same way.

We went on to meet my other streams of kids in their classrooms, interrupting classes in geography, physics, and mathematics. The teachers didn't seem to mind, as they also wanted to meet me. I had to learn where all the classrooms were, as I would have to find them on my own the next day.

My first day turned out to be an orientation of sorts. Melchior took me to the Language Arts office, a small building behind the main campus, and went over the plan for the semester that I had painstakingly crafted, using a ruler I purchased at the office supply shop to make columns and rows for all the dates and descriptions to go in the boxes. I would have loved to type it, but the only computer at the school was in the administration office for the sole use of the Principal and his assistant. It had a cable connection and no Wi-Fi.

After Melchior signed off on my plan for the semester, we discussed the school and the students.

"Only primary education is free in this country, so sending a child to Secondary School can be a huge sacrifice," he said. "We used to let the students keep coming to school if the parents fell behind in the payments, but now they have to leave if the fees aren't paid by the end of each quarter. The students in Form 1 English are usually thirteen to fifteen years old, but some have been out of school for a while or failed exams and were kept back. Some of your students are almost twenty.

"The parents have to pay for uniforms and books, also," he continued. "That's why you will see a lot of uniforms that look old or don't fit. They have been passed down from other relatives. And that's why we don't require a lot of books. They're too expensive." He looked at me inquiringly, probably wondering if this was going to be a problem for me.

"Don't worry," I said. "When I got my certificate to teach English as a foreign language, I was taught to teach without books. They are a luxury in a lot of places."

"I'm happy to hear that," he said. "Most American teachers I have met are used to having a lot of supplies to work with and have a hard time."

"I would probably be the same way, but I got my certificate in South America," I told him. "I brought my laptop so I can get lesson plans off the internet or make up my own."

"You are not going to find Wi-Fi here," Melchior advised. "There are a couple of shops in town where you can rent time, but their computers are old and slow. A lot of times their internet is down."

"Ashley told us to buy computer modems in Dar es Salaam. Will they work here?" I asked, hoping I hadn't wasted forty dollars on the modem and initial data plan. It seemed to work fine when I tried it out in Dar.

"You will be lucky to get a connection," he said. "Most of the office workers in town use modems and take up all the bandwidth available here. You'll have better luck late at night or near dawn, when the offices are closed and people aren't using their own computers in the evening."

This did not bode well for me, since my "teach without a book" strategy relied heavily on getting lesson plans, educational games, and the like from the internet. I did not feel experienced enough or sure enough of my memory of grammar rules to make stuff up off the top of my head. I wished that I had brought a simple grammar book from home for reference.

I was learning not to rely on Ashley's assurances after the ATM and Wi-Fi disappointments. Her promise to visit in two weeks also became a fantasy. She had a whole country full of volunteers to oversee, and apparently assumed some things because she didn't have the time or resources to personally check out all the volunteer sites. If a town had an ATM or internet, she assumed they were available to everyone. I would have to rely more on myself and not depend on her to solve my problems.

Melchior took me to the teachers' lounge and introduced

me to some of the teachers I hadn't met yet. The students served a very nice hot tea, and he treated me to a *mendazi*, a small doughnut-like pastry that the students sold every day at teatime to make money for the school's extracurricular programs. Everyone was very welcoming and spoke to me in English.

I was surprised by the variety of clothing they wore. Most of the men wore slacks and sweaters, but the women dressed according to cultural preferences. Mama Rose, the geography teacher, was married to a lawyer and wore Western-style dresses that came below her knee. The other two women I met wore ankle-length dresses but were very different in style. Juliana, Melchior's wife, wore colorful African print dresses with turbans to match. Mrs. Walter, a Muslim, wore long, gauzy dresses, jackets, and headscarves.

All of the students wore turquoise V-neck sweaters over white button-up shirts with collars and short or long sleeves. The males and the Muslim girls wore black pants. The rest of the girls wore calf-length, pleated, kelly-green skirts. I often saw them tugging up their skirts and tightening the safety pins that made the hand-me-down skirts fit. I never asked if they envied the Muslim girls' religious exclusion that allowed them to wear pants to cover their legs and scarves to cover their bald heads.

That afternoon, I observed some of the other teachers at work. The students seemed to enjoy the classes and were eager to learn. I witnessed a few dramatic moments when fingers were swatted with thin wooden switches for small infractions like talking in class or not being prepared.

"Why do you hit the children?" I asked Mama Rose after she dismissed her class.

"It is the way we do things here," she replied. "It is the

way they learn. If that child learns the lesson, she may never be hit again."

"It just seems cruel," I said.

"Well, we learned it from you," she snickered. "The Europeans taught us well."

"When I was a child, I got spanked if I was naughty," I replied. "I don't think many parents do that anymore. I know American schools used to use physical discipline, and some might still do so. I just don't hear about it anymore."

"We don't do it nearly as much or as harshly as we used to, either," she reflected. "Some schoolmasters get very physical, especially with the older boys. Our principal likes to use soft discipline. He often embarrasses them by making them do the chicken walk through the center of campus, or something like that. It might even work better. They often end up laughing at the end as they race to see who can finish first."

I felt pretty good about my first day at school and went over my lesson plan for the next day in my head as I walked home from school. I immediately changed gears as I arrived home and found Anna crying. She had already been teaching for a week and seemed happy with the school, the students, and the other teachers.

"What's wrong?" I asked. "Did something happen at school?"

"It was horrible!" she exclaimed. "One of my students asked to go to the bathroom. The Vice Principal saw him and accused him of skipping class. I heard some yelling and looked outside. Two teachers were holding the student down on the ground while the Vice Principal kicked him in the side of his body! I went out to see what was wrong and they told me to go back inside. I tried to stop him and he yelled at me! I never want to see that man again!"

Ashley had warned us that hitting was accepted discipline in Tanzanian schools. I thought the light finger slapping with switches that I observed was bad enough, but kicking a student while he was being held down on the floor seemed like way too much. Anna obviously thought so too.

"Talk to your Principal tomorrow when you go to school," I advised her. "Tell him you approved the student to leave the room."

"I told the Vice Principal and he ignored me!"

"Talk to the Principal. See if this is unusual in that school. If it isn't, you may have to talk to Mama Caritas," I told her.

"I think I'll call her anyway," Anna said. "I don't think I can get past this."

In the end, Anna was accused of violating her chain of command by talking to Mama Caritas before she met with her Principal. The Vice Principal was reprimanded for not investigating before he punished the student, but not for the punishment itself. Anna was told the student was ashamed and was transferring to another school but she was never able to verify that. Anna told me she avoided the Vice Principal from that day on and seldom had interactions with him. During the semester, she witnessed and heard about other beatings, some involving fists and feet, and protested when she felt she could.

I was thankful my Principal seemed more enlightened about punishment and eventually talked to him about it.

"I was a small child, and the other boys would sometimes pick on me," he reflected. "They stopped when I got bigger than they were. But then the teachers seemed to see me as a threat and sometimes beat me for no reason. When I became a teacher, I told myself I would be different. Sometimes my size alone is enough to make people stop and think. I don't get involved too much if other teachers feel discipline is necessary, and there are limits on how harsh they can be. I try to encourage a better way."

I thought back to my own childhood and the few times I had been spanked. It seemed acceptable back in the 1950s, and I heard "Spare the rod, spoil the child" more than once. The one time I got frustrated enough to try to spank my own son when he was about five, he just laughed and looked at me like, "Is that all you've got?"

I just don't have it in me, and I know my son would probably never even think of spanking my grandson. I don't think it means we are weak. We just understand, like my Principal, that there are better ways to get your point across.

I had no control over whether my students were punished in other classes, and I sometimes got teased for being too weak to do it myself. It came to a head one day when I let my brightest stream of students, who were ahead of the others on my schedule, have a debate class as a special treat.

Apparently there used to be a debate club at the school, but the teacher who sponsored it transferred to another town. I wanted to encourage the students to consider both sides of an issue, so it sounded like a good idea. I had never been exposed to debates in school, but the students seemed to know the structure and process. I gave them a list of topics and examples of arguments, and encouraged them to debate on the side opposite of what they would normally pick.

The students formed three debate groups, each with two teams of three students debating opposite sides of their chosen topic. The teams got together and came up with arguments for their side of the issue. They then decided who would present each argument, making sure everyone got to participate. One student was chosen to be the moderator of the debates and the rest of the class served as judges. I sat in the front row of the "jury" as an impartial observer. The moderator sat at the teacher's desk facing the room, with team's opposing sides in desks on either side of him.

We started out with the topic "Payment of a Bride Price is Outdated." A team of boys argued that the traditional dowry paid to the bride's family made it harder for them to afford to take care of a family. Unsurprisingly, an all-girls team took the negative side, arguing that their families deserved to be compensated for money spent on their education. The judges, mostly girls, decided that the girls' team won the debate. The boys grumbled, but then sat down to take their turn as judges.

The debate topic "Corporal Punishment Should Be Allowed in Schools" was a lot more heated. I doubted any of the students agreed with the premise, but both teams did a good job putting forth their arguments. There were some raised voices as the boys bantered back and forth, smiling. I could tell they were really enjoying the debate from their grins. The judges cheered them on.

All of a sudden the classroom door opened. Mama Rose stood there, switch in hand, scanning the room with a hard look on her face, as if seeking troublemakers. The students seemed to freeze. She finally saw me sitting in one of the student desks in the front row.

"Is everything okay?" she asked warily.

"We're just having a debate," I answered, wondering what she thought had happened. Did she think the students had killed their *mzungu* teacher? "Were we making too much noise?"

"I was in the classroom next door and I heard yelling. I wanted to make sure you weren't having trouble."

"No, we're fine," I replied. "I'll try to have them keep the noise down."

Chastened, the debaters gave their final arguments in

softer tones. As expected, the judges agreed that corporal punishment should not be allowed in schools.

The final team debated the topic "Students Should Wear Uniforms." Again, it was girls versus boys. They were having fun with their arguments, some of them silly, and voices got increasingly louder and giddier. Distracted by the arguments, I forgot to warn them to keep the noise down. There was a loud crash as the door suddenly banged against the wall.

"What's going on here?" growled Edgar, the math teacher, as he surveyed the room with a menacing gleam in his eyes. I had never talked to him before, but his large frame and threatening demeanor reminded me of a bully. I noticed he was carrying a long stick that was sturdy enough to do some serious damage if applied to a human body. I hated confrontation, especially with someone who walked around carrying a club, but I didn't want him focusing on any of my students.

I quickly stood and walked to the door, putting myself in his direct line of vision. I didn't think he would beat another teacher. At least, I had never heard of that happening.

"Sorry if we were making too much noise," I said loudly, to compensate for my shaking limbs. "We're having a debate."

"A debate?" he roared. "That's not in the syllabus."

"In America we use debate to reinforce lessons," I improvised. "Thank you for checking on us. I'll try to keep the noise down." I stepped forward to back him out the door and swiftly closed it as he snarled, "Make sure you do."

I turned to survey my students. Their expressions changed rapidly from fear to relief to smiles. "Let's finish this debate," I said, as I walked back to my chair.

"Yes, Mama Mary," they shouted as they grinned and resumed their places.

More subdued, we finished quickly and put the desks

back in their original spots. In the time left, I asked for opinions on how the debates went. Everyone agreed they had gone well, with good arguments on both sides.

"I never thought there was a good argument for corporal punishment, but they almost convinced me," laughed Mohammed.

"There's a good argument for everything. You just have to look at both sides and decide which you think is best," I said. "Don't just go along with everyone else. Look at the pros and cons and make your own decision."

I decided that the debates had been a good experience, for them and for me. They had learned to think logically, and I had stood up to a bully, and won.

7

MWANZA

Behind every dark storm is a bright rainbow.

— MATSHONA DHILWAYO

---

*W*e had decent running water and electricity for the first month. Mama Caritas, always well turned out in long tailored dresses in African prints with headscarves to match, continued to promise us a stove, hot running water, and mosquito nets. We continued to wait.

I had to take off work several times to wait for the plumber to come and install hot water in our shower. I was lucky if he even came the day he was expected, and he always had excuses, sometimes threatening that nothing would happen unless I gave him some extra money on the side. Our problems seemed to grow as the plumber delayed.

- "Well, it doesn't work because some animal chewed up the wiring and you need to get a new water heater."
- "Well, you can't get a new water heater until the council meets and approves the new budget, maybe next month."
- "Well, you have water all over the floor in the kitchen because the pipes broke," the same pipes he had fixed right before we moved in but hadn't fastened together.
- "Well, the shower and water heater are in but the water tank for the compound is empty and the pump in town is broken so no telling when there will be more water."
- "Well, the toilet won't flush because the septic tank is backed up."
- "Well, the toilet backs up into the shower because you need a new septic line."

Cold water was the norm in a country where only fourteen percent of the households had electricity. We had electric lights, but they only functioned if there was no power outage or if the compound manager, who also had a full-time government job requiring frequent travel, remembered to put money in the meter. The compound was usually well lit, with floodlights covering most of it.

If there was no power, the black void of the African night distorted senses of balance and distance and made the three-mile morning walk to school in the dark problematic, even with a flashlight. My students seemed to have no problem walking miles from their farms in the dark to get to school. It made me wonder if, living our privileged life in the United

States, the special sense that helps us navigate in the dark has been bred out of us.

Things got a little better after we met our neighbor, Ray, an Englishman who lived in comparative luxury in a house in the compound that had a regular stove and oven, refrigerator, hot water, shower, television, *and* a view. Ray worked for Concern, an Irish international charity that provided clean water for needy communities around the world. He was the only foreigner in the Ngara office. They paid for his house and furnishings, but he had to let them use it occasionally for conferences. When he first arrived, the other employees had driven him to Mwanza several times to get things, including a bicycle.

Ray's house had two large bedrooms and two bathrooms, and his living room and porches were enormous. He must have felt sorry for us, because he gave us his extra key so we could use his second bathroom and shower.

The best thing Ray had was a four-quart electric kettle. After greedily drinking water from one of his colorful, unmatched coffee cups, Anna grimaced and said, "It still kind of tastes like dirt."

"It's not filtered, but I'm telling you, it's safe to drink, and I'm an expert!" he said, watching our doubtful faces. "This is Africa!"

We boiled some more water and took it back to our house in a thermos. That weekend, we walked to town and bought our own large electric kettle to heat water for drinking, cooking, and washing. We could only find a two-quart size, but it saved us from hours of trying to heat water on the kerosene stove in a saucepan, constantly looking to see if it was boiling. Not to mention the hundreds of plastic bottles we didn't have to buy and burn. Anna found a five-gallon styrofoam container with a spigot on the bottom that we could store boiled water in. We got into a routine of boiling water at night to fill up the container. In the morning, we had cool water to fill up our water bottles before we headed off to school. We were pleased to note that the water tasted better because a lot of the sediment drifted to the bottom of the container, below the spigot, as it sat and cooled overnight.

A couple of weeks after arriving in Ngara, we still had no stove, mosquito net, or shower, but our beloved electric tea kettle gave us hot water for drinking, coffee, and sink baths. We also found some packages of ramen in the "supermarket" so we could easily make noodles. Anna took advantage of Ray's kitchen one night and made a fabulous green banana curry. She tasked Ray and me with making chapatis out of flour and water and they came out surprisingly well. We agreed that it was the best dinner we had had so far.

We gradually got more variety in our diet. We made spaghetti at Ray's and ate dinner a few times at the Afriline canteen. Although it seemed moribund in the daytime, things perked up there at night, with music and even occasional dancing. They always served the same thing: rice, beans, spinach, and meat. Most of the meat was not very edible, either stringy and tough or all fat and bone, but the sauce tasted good on rice. When the "meat" was dried fish, I passed on it, because I couldn't stand looking at the fish heads. Our breakfast was usually a peanut butter and banana sandwich. Both of our schools served the teachers tea and small doughnuts, or *mendazi*, on lunch breaks.

We were far removed from the "anything at anytime" availability of goods in the developed world. The "supermarket" in town was like a mini-Walmart compressed into one dark room about twenty by forty feet and filled with industrial shelving. Most of the room was taken up by sundries and hardware, but there were a few shelves of packaged food like boxed juice, cookies, powdered milk, oil, mustard, coffee, and spices.

The owner was from Oman, and most of the items were imported from Arab countries. She also sold small loaves of white bread from a local baker for about eighty cents, but they always tasted stale, even when bought right after delivery. I never saw any other kind of bread in Tanzania, except for some whole grain rolls I bought at a restaurant in Mwanza. I doubt the bread was fortified with vitamins like in the U.S., but it was filling. Rice and white flour were available but expensive compared to other things, about a dollar per kilogram.

The family that owned the supermarket also owned Paradise, the best restaurant in town. The Omanis approved all the recipes and a local woman supervised the cooking. There was no menu but they offered a daily buffet of rice, fried bananas, beef stew, tomato sauce, and cabbage salad for about two dollars. Sometimes they offered chicken, which was nicely prepared but still seemed like skin on bone with no meat.

The other restaurants in town were basically shops with a few tables and no running water. We enjoyed an outdoor bar named Garden Pause, where people gathered to drink beer in little cabanas roofed with thatch. On an irregular basis, they also offered rice, meat stew, grilled meat on skewers, and *chips mayai,* a Tanzanian omelette made with french fries and eggs. I sometimes stopped there on the way home from school, but rarely at night because I could not walk home in the dark. The lack of ambient light was a little scary, although we weren't aware of a big local crime problem. We just felt that *mzungus* were targets.

On the plus side, we had access to a plethora of fresh vegetables at comparatively cheap prices, even with the "*mzungo* premium" we sometimes had to pay. Besides the central market in town, there were some open-air stalls only a twenty-minute walk from home, where our dirt road met the main road.

The best prices were at the Saturday market, when all kinds of sellers brought their goods, fruits, vegetables, meat, used clothes, shoes, and *kangas* (lengths of African print material used for clothes and a lot of other things), and laid them out on blankets for display. It covered a whole hillside and was only a five-minute walk from our house. Purchasing anything there involved some bargaining, which became easier after learning the going price range for things. A kilogram of potatoes (about a half pound) was forty cents, an avocado was twelve cents and a small pineapple about thirty cents. Eggs, if you could find them, were about fifteen cents apiece. Life was good on Saturdays.

We ate meat rarely and only at restaurants, since we had no refrigerator. Even there I usually avoided it, since the goat and beef meat was very tough and took a long time to chew. Often, I chewed for a while for the flavor and spit what was left into my napkin because it never softened. The chickens had so little meat on them it was almost not worth the trouble. The goats I passed on the way home from school were extremely skinny, which told me the restaurants weren't just trying to cheat the *mzungus* with inferior food.

Farmers occasionally brought live chickens to school to sell to the teachers for about three dollars apiece. One of the teachers offered to come to my house and slaughter a chicken for me, but I refused, since I had no idea what to do with it and was not sure I wanted to learn. Anna did not have the same qualms. She bought a chicken and kept it in a pen near

87

the canteen to fatten it up for a few weeks. Then two of her fellow teachers came over to help her kill and defeather the chicken. They laughed at her squeamishness throughout the process.

"You'll never be an African woman," they told her as they left.

The canteen let Anna use their kitchen to cook the bird. She put hot stones in the bottom of a soup pot and put the chicken in with a little water and spices before covering it with the lid. She then put it on a burner on low heat and cooked it for about two hours. We had Ray and three other guests for dinner that night and each got about a tablespoon's worth of chicken.

"This tastes great!" I told her. "You'll have to do this again."

"Not in this life," she answered.

A few weeks later, we finally got some days off to go to Mwanza, the second largest city in Tanzania. It sits on the shores of Lake Victoria, the largest lake in Africa. We were excited to see it, but moaning about the dreaded ten-hour bus ride on a mix of paved and dirt roads, when Ray, our savior, said, "No worries. Some of the staff are going to Mwanza in the company's Toyota Land Cruiser. I'll see if they have room."

Thus Ray, Anna, and I ended up having a long weekend away in Mwanza, with its large markets, international restaurants, and multiple ATMs.

After finally getting some cash, we had a good time shopping in the market and eating "real" food. We pigged out as we stimulated our taste buds with Chinese and Indian meals and pizza! One of my favorite finds was fresh cucumbers, which I had not seen in Ngara. I had never considered them one of my favorite foods, but they tasted like heaven when peeled and sprinkled with salt and pepper. Carts parked along the street sold them chilled, with one end wrapped in a napkin so they stuck out like an ice cream cone.

Finally, we headed for a lakeside lodge where the truck would meet us to take us home.

"Do we have time for a swim?" I asked Ray, looking longingly at the inviting calm blue water of the lake.

"You don't want to swim in Lake Victoria," he replied. "The water snail larvae will get into your bloodstream and make you sick. It's called Bilharzia, or Schistosomiasis."

"I've heard of that." I shuddered. "You're right, I don't want that."

"Snail larvae sound gross," added Anna, scrunching up her freckled face.

It was a bad omen that our water was off Thursday when we left Ngara and still off Sunday night when we returned. Mama Caritas called to tell us that the water tank at Afriline was empty. She had arranged for a plumber to come out the next day to put in our shower, but he couldn't do anything if there was no running water. On the bright side, she said the stove was coming soon.

After six weeks of anticipation, the "stove" turned out to be a two-burner hot plate. We gave up our dream of baking peanut butter cookies. The hot plate turned out to be fine unless the electricity went out in the middle of cooking. That event was rare when we first moved in, but increased in frequency.

We had already resigned ourselves to living without a refrigerator. Warm beer and powdered milk were the norm there. Leftovers might last overnight on the countertop, but after that they were history, unless you wanted to risk some serious stomach upset. Lack of refrigeration meant that meat and poultry were pretty much not on the menu. There were barrels of black, dried fish in the markets, but the bulging eyes made them unappetizing to me.

The mosquito nets we finally got were for king-sized beds, but instead of coming down from a central hook, they were made for a four-poster bed. Our beds didn't have frames. Mama Caritas refused to return the nets, since they had come from Dar es Salaam. They ended up in the closet, and I continued to pull the sheet over my head at night. What happened after I went to sleep I left up to the gods. I was just thankful I hadn't seen any spiders since the week we moved in.

Anna seemed to attract small visitors. One day, after coming home from school, she changed into loose gray sweatpants and a T-shirt to get more comfortable before sitting down in our living room to correct homework. Suddenly, she jumped up and started gyrating her hips in what looked like a crazy dance. Her nose wrinkled and her eyes closed. I thought she might be doing some form of exercise.

"What are you doing?" I asked, as I looked up from the book I was reading.

"I have an itch," she explained. She reached her hand behind her and yelped.

"What's wrong?" I demanded, worried that she hurt herself by twisting too much.

"Something's in here with me," she cried, as she dropped her sweatpants to her ankles.

A small gecko tumbled to the floor and sped up the nearby wall. Anna stood frozen as she watched it for a moment, then broke into a laugh.

"I hate that he invaded my space, but I don't want to get

rid of him because I hate mosquitoes more. I hope he eats a ton of them."

A few days later, Anna had an even more unwelcome visitor. Investigating an unusual noise one night, I noticed her tossing and turning on the living room couch.

"Can't sleep?" I inquired.

"I probably could, but I woke up and there was a huge rat on my bed," she huffed. I noticed the door to her room was shut. I had no desire to open it and verify her claim. It was the middle of the night and I wanted to go back to sleep.

"Well, try to get some sleep and we'll see what we can do in the morning," I said, as I walked back to my room and shut the door. I shut my closet door also, hoping there was no hole connecting her room and mine that would let the unwanted interloper in.

Three days later, Anna was still sleeping on the couch. The rat had refused to leave, and cheekily ignored the poisoned food and traps set out to hasten his demise. Anna came home from school and declared that the Vice Principal was coming to kill the creature.

"I'm surprised you asked him," I said. "Isn't he your nemesis?"

"I asked some of the others, and he's the only one who would come," she replied. "Besides, who is better suited to clobber someone's brains out?"

"Maybe he's trying to make amends," I said.

"No, I think he just likes hurting things." She looked down at the floor, maybe thinking of the way he had hurt some of her students. A knock at the door brought her out of her reverie. The Vice Principal sauntered in, carrying a big stick. I stayed by her side to offer support and protection. I didn't notice any conversation or even eye contact between them. She just pointed to her bedroom door, and he went in and shut it behind him. A few minutes later, we heard a few whacks, a high pitched squeal, then silence. The Vice Principal came out of the bedroom holding his stick in one hand and a huge rat dangling from its tail in the other. Anna nodded and, still wordlessly, both of her nemeses were soon gone.

That same afternoon, we were sitting on the porch when one of the compound's security guards walked by carrying a box with mewling sounds coming from within. "Wait," Anna called out. "What do you have in there?"

"One of the feral cats had a litter of kittens but she got hit by a car yesterday," he replied somberly. "I'm taking them to the dump to dispose of them."

"Oh, no!" Anna cried out. "How can you do that?"

Misunderstanding, he said, "It's very fast and easy. They are too young to put up a fight. I just twist their necks."

Soft-hearted Anna was not letting him go. "Let me see," she asked.

Six ginger and white kittens, scrambling over each other in the box, continued their mewling as we inspected them. Their age was undetermined, but they looked too young to be away from their mother.

Anna picked one up and said, "This one is mine and its name is Poa. I need a rat catcher."

The guard laughed, saying, "The rats here are much bigger than that cat. They might be the ones chasing him." But he continued on his way, leaving Anna with a new friend.

Anna was already exhausted from three days of dealing with the rat. Her new kitten was not ready to be weaned yet, so she took a disposable plastic glove she had brought from home for some unknown reason and made a makeshift nipple. I looked on dubiously, having never been a cat lover. I had a dog as a child, but Anna's mother had several cats. This cat was effectively my new roommate.

"Why did you name it Poa?" I asked.

"Poa means 'cool' in Swahili. He is destined to be a cool cat," she said, stroking the kitten repeatedly as he tried to suckle. "Don't worry. I'll take care of it and you won't even know it's here."

That, of course, was ridiculous, as cats are independent creatures and seem to take over wherever they reside. They also have to pee and poop and cough up hairballs, sometimes where you don't expect them too. All this was in the future, though, as I looked at the furry ball and reached out a finger to touch it.

After all, who can resist a kitten?

~

The next week, Ashley called from her cell phone in Dar. "Guess what?" she exclaimed. "You will be so excited!"

"I can't imagine," I replied. All kinds of thoughts were whirling around my head, the foremost being that our water situation was fixed, but none of them turned out to be right.

Helen Claire, the Director of WorldTeach, who was in charge of the programs in all twenty countries they operated in, was coming to Africa to meet with the government of Rwanda to formalize details for starting the program there. On Wednesday, she would come to Ngara for one night. This was an honor, since we were the only volunteer site in Africa she was visiting. We had only been there a couple of months, and I wondered if we would be able to make her proud.

We wanted to clean up our house for her, but, alas, the water service went out again so we could only sweep the floors. Thank goodness Anna's cat, Poa, had started going to the bathroom in the tile shower instead of on the living room rug, or worse, right in front of my bedroom door so I would step in it first thing in the morning. One day he joined Anna in the bathroom and did his thing at the same time as her. He often repeated that, so he must have learned where to go by example. Having cats go to the bathroom in your shower does not sound hygienic, but the shower was preferable to the rest of the house, and easier to clean up. The shower hadn't worked since we had been there, anyway. We had been heating up a small bucket of water and standing in the shower to bathe, letting the water go down the drain. If there was running water, I would use Ray's extra shower about once a week to wash my hair and body more thoroughly.

Ashley told us that Helen Claire and one of the American donors were coming with a rented car and driver and would arrive around 6 p.m. so she could see our house before having dinner in the canteen at 7:30. We did not have her phone number so were unable to call her to verify that. The plan fizzled when they didn't arrive when expected.

Helen Claire later told us that their car broke down at the Rwanda border. They were able to get it going again, but it broke down again right next to the Ngara petrol station, where they were supposed to meet Anna to guide them to Afriline. Helen Claire said she tried to call Anna six times while en route, but her cell phone apparently could not connect in the rural area.

They saw the neon lights of the petrol station right before the power in the whole town went out. Everything was suddenly pitch black, except for the gorgeous stars in the sky. They were finally able to reach Anna by cell phone. She got the prearranged *piky piky* to take her to the station so she could show the visitors the way to our compound. There was apparently some discussion about leaving one person behind so the car was not unattended, but Anna convinced them that the crime rate was low and the car would be fine.

They showed up at Afriline in a taxi around 8:45 p.m. and went directly to the canteen. They never saw our house. The prepared dinner was definitely on the cold side, but everyone was hungry enough to do it justice. It was even kind of romantic, since we had to eat by candlelight. But the visitors were tired and in a rush to get to their "hotel." After about twenty minutes of desultory conversation, Afriline staff grabbed some flashlights and took them to the pitch-black house provided for them.

The power was on the next morning, but there was still no running water. Anna met Helen Claire and her companion, Susan, and took them to her school. Her students had prepared a little "Welcome Helen Claire" speech that was apparently well received.

The visitors then came to Ngara Secondary School and met me. I had kept my C-stream students for an extra period, hoping to impress them with my teaching, but they arrived about fifteen minutes after I finished. The lesson had been about Occupations and included the students playing a lively guessing game of "What's My Line?"

All my writing was still on the wall when I took them to visit the class. I was glad they didn't witness the class on Character Traits the week before. When I had asked the class to name their heroes, several named Barack Obama, but just as many said Osama Bin Laden. I didn't think that would go over well with the donor.

The students had a free period and, in contrast to the organized reception Helen Claire and Susan got in Anna's class, they were swarmed by the students. After I finally got them to sit down and be introduced, Helen Claire commented on what a "challenge" they were. I then took the visitors to see the library and one of my other classes, also in a free period but not so rambunctious.

Helen Claire, Susan and I were all using cameras and that seemed to get the kids really excited, maybe because they rarely had an opportunity to get their pictures taken. I organized group pictures out on the grass, but afterwards heard lots of calls of, "Take me! Take me!" as they made silly poses. Nobody really misbehaved, but they were definitely overenthusiastic, and it was frustrating to try to keep them in line. Nonetheless, I hoped the visitors were charmed.

Helen Claire seemed preoccupied but Susan, the American donor, took me aside before they left and said, "I couldn't do what you're doing." I could have taken that either way, but I chose to see it as a positive comment, praising my taking on the job, and not my poor control of the kids.

Ashley later told us Helen Claire had nothing but praise for us, but hadn't expected the hard living conditions.

"That's because her timing was off the whole time she was here," I replied. "She arrived in the dark and never got to see our nice house, she ate a cold dinner because she was late, and she had trouble getting settled because she had never seen the house she stayed at in daylight and only had a flashlight to find her way around. I'm disappointed that she only got to see my students when they were on break and running around. They are good kids, but I think she got a bad impression of them."

"You're wrong," said Ashley. "She said she has traveled all over the world with her work and is used to things not going as planned. She described your kids as eager and excited, and that they seemed to like and respect you."

"I couldn't ask for more," I said, humbled that the visit wasn't the total fiasco I thought it was. Maybe I wasn't such a failure as a teacher after all.

Notwithstanding all the drawbacks, the place was starting to feel like home. I felt like I was adapting well and successfully meeting all of the challenges my surroundings were throwing at me. Despite being a woman "of a certain age," I was quietly celebrating walking through new doors and, for the most part, enjoying whatever new adventures they led to.

I looked forward to whatever came next.

8

HOTEL RWANDA REVISITED

Strange, I thought, how you can be living your dreams
and your nightmares at the very same time.

— RANSOM RIGGS, *HOLLOW CITY*

I was fascinated by Rwanda when I visited there as
part of a trans-Africa tour in 1975. I fondly
remembered the beautiful green hills and friendly people. In
the late 1990s, it caught my attention for a much different
reason. The whole population seemed to be killing each
other. In the end, a million people, almost twenty percent of
the population, died in what was called the Genocide.

Now I was living in Ngara, just across the Tanzanian
border from Rwanda. In the 1990s, Ngara was the United
Nations Headquarters for handling the Genocide. We were
living in their old housing outside of town, and I could see
the border from my housemate's school.

The coming Monday would be a school holiday for

"Farmers' Day." I decided to use the long weekend to go to Kigali, the capital of neighboring Rwanda, for some respite from our lack of cooking facilities and running water, as well as the more recent trials with the rat and the cat. My house-mate, Anna, had planned to go with me, but decided she wanted to stay home and rehabilitate her room before moving back in. She planned to scrub and paint the whole thing, removing any evidence of the whiskered hooligan that had taken over her room for several days.

"Will you be okay here by yourself?" I asked dubiously. She was well over twenty-one, but I had thirty-five years on her and felt somewhat responsible.

"No problem," she answered. "We live in a gated compound with a guard. If I have any issues, I'll call the guards or my Vice Principal to beat whoever it is up." Her grin told me she wasn't concerned, so I felt better about leaving her behind. I had some qualms about traveling to another country by myself, but decided to go anyway.

On Saturday morning, one of my neighbors gave me a ride to the Ngara "bus station." We passed the downtown shacks that served as shops and the two huge old U.N. tents that housed the central market. The buses sat in an adjacent dirt lot about the size of a football field.

There were buses a few days a week north to Mwanza and east to the coast, but none to Rwanda. To get there, you had to take a taxi to the border, go through immigration and customs, then take another taxi or bus to Kigali, about a six-hour trip one way.

Most of the taxi drivers in town were independent contractors and the taxis were beaten up old Toyota Corollas. When I say old, I mean twenty or thirty years, usually discards that had used up their shelf life in the First World but started a whole new life in Africa. The taxis sat in clusters.

There were no signs. I walked up to one that looked a little less disreputable than the rest and had three people in the back seat.

"Are you going to Rwanda?" I asked the driver. "Yes," he grinned wolfishly. "Forty thousand shillings special rate."

I quickly did the math and figured this was about $26, which sounded like a *mzungu* price and probably far more than the people already in the taxi were going to pay. I looked around and asked some of the other drivers what they would charge. They agreed with the stated price until one man sitting on a motorcycle told me it should be about ten thousand shillings. I looked around at the other drivers, hoping one of them would agree to that rate. I got blank stares until a middle aged man in faded, dusty clothes said the price was $26 if I went by myself, but a shared taxi would be three thousand shillings to the transfer point at Bumati, where I would have to get another taxi for three thousand shillings to the border.

"Perfect," I breathed as I climbed into the front passenger seat of his Toyota. Meanwhile, he kept stuffing more and more people into the back until there were five adults and three children in the back seat, two in the hatchback space, and a teenage girl sharing my bucket seat in the front. We were off, and it wasn't too bad until the driver picked up two more people along the way and ended up sharing his seat with a teenage boy, reaching around the tangle of legs to get to the gear shift. I whispered the *mzungo* curse, "TIA," as I thought about the useless, shredded seatbelt dangling from the side of my seat.

We finally got to the transfer point, which was another dirt lot with more old cars sitting adjacent to a bus stop. I asked around and found a 1980 Toyota Corolla going to the border. After about twenty minutes of sitting patiently in the car, I asked the driver, "Can we go?"

"No," he replied, looking at me calmly. "I need at least five people."

"What if I pay you more?" I queried.

"No, I need at least five people." A bus soon came and disgorged some bodies, and we soon left with five adults and two children in the back seat, plus an adorable toddler with a runny nose on my lap in the front.

The road got more steep as we climbed into the mountains. Soon I noticed smoke coming out of the dashboard and a burning smell.

"You'd better stop and see what's wrong," I implored the driver, trying to keep the panic from my voice.

"Oil leaky," he calmly replied, but finally stopped the car and got out, walking around to the back. I thought he was checking the car, but he just picked up three more people and put them in the hatchback space.

My first thought was to get out and wait for another car to come along, but we had only seen a couple of farm trucks in the last hour, and I didn't want to get stuck in the middle of nowhere overnight. I resorted to silent prayer.

About twenty minutes later, we reached the border between Rwanda and Tanzania, a river notable for a huge waterfall that promised endless water. I thought of our near constant struggle to get delivery of buckets of water, and it looked like a slice of heaven. I felt like I had made it to the Promised Land.

After Rwanda immigration, I saw a row of newer white minibuses and found out that they went to Kigali on a regular schedule, about every hour. The trip took three hours, with a few brief stops. People got on and off but there was plenty of room for everyone to have a seat.

I watched the land going by out the window and felt I was indeed in another country, very mountainous and green. The cows and goats were much fatter than the skin-and-bones animals I had seen in Tanzania, and the houses looked more prosperous and substantial. I saw several "U.S. Aid for International Development Project" signs along the road.

The only hotel I knew the name of in Kigali was the Mille Collines, famous from the 2004 Academy Award nominated movie, *Hotel Rwanda*, based on a true story in which the hotel manager hid hundreds of people from the killers stalking the city during the Genocide. I asked to go there and the driver let me off at a multi-story hotel and pointed, "There."

It was not the Mille Collines, but at this point I was ready to settle. My Visa credit card was useless in Tanzania but the hotel staff in Rwanda didn't bat an eye. Two nights there cost more than my $200 stipend for the month, but at this point I didn't care. I just wanted to shower, wash my hair, and eat some good food.

My room on the sixth floor had a view of the city lights, a flat screen TV, and free high speed Wi-Fi. After a long shower and washing my hair twice, I headed to the hotel restaurant. It was late afternoon, and I was the only one there. I looked at the white tablecloths and the sharply dressed staff and felt I was in the wrong place, somehow, and had arrived there by mistake. That didn't stop me from sitting down and ordering chicken curry and a huge green salad. I tried not to compare the large, succulent pieces of chicken in a divine sauce with meals in Ngara, where eating chicken was like sucking bones, and beef was so stringy it took ten minutes to chew.

Later, I got a text from Anna telling me she had a headache and joint pain, and was at the hospital having tests.

"U OK?" I texted back.

"No problem. Kerry and Laura are coming from Rulenge to visit tomorrow and will make sure I'm OK," she replied.

I was glad she would have someone to check on her, so I continued my visit unconcerned after doing a mental check on my own health status. The main change was that I felt pleasantly full. I remembered that both Anna and I had diarrhea earlier in the week, but that was not unusual in that time and place. Also, I had been taking antibiotics for a bad burn on my leg from an uncovered *piky piky* exhaust pipe that had left a huge, weeping blister from my ankle halfway to my knee. Maybe the medicine had protected me from whatever was wrong with her.

I went upstairs to check out the disco, which had a three-hundred-sixty degree view of the city and its many parks and high rise buildings, so different from the cities in Tanzania I had seen. Millions of dollars had flowed into Rwanda since the Genocide. I think a lot of that was due to guilt because the world was so slow to step in and do anything about the massacre. The Rwandan government, which itself was not blameless, couldn't get anything done unless everyone got past it. There was a blanket amnesty because much of the population was involved on one side or the other.

The Genocide was a very brutal time, when the tribe in power basically set out to exterminate another tribe favored by the former colonists, even though the tribes by that time lived together peacefully and often intermarried. Secret "Kill lists" had been made up ahead of time, filed away, while young people were recruited and trained to perform the systematic slaughter with guns and machetes. The mysterious death of the Rwandan President in a plane crash became the signal to start the genocide. A local radio station told listeners to "fill the graves." Criminals with AIDS were released from confinement and directed to infect the unwanted population. The rampant killings convulsed the country for 100 days.

Almost twenty years later, it still felt creepy to walk around the city and look into faces of people who were probably around at that time. I wondered what their role had been, if they had been part of the "kill squads" of teenagers sent out to bludgeon people to death or whack them with machetes, and how they could go on after that as if nothing had happened.

I visited the Kigali Genocide Memorial Center and heard the recorded voices of the radio at the time, encouraging people to either hide or, conversely, to get out and join the fray. I walked on concrete walkways built over the mass graves of over 250,000 people that were put to rest there. I felt like I had to tiptoe so as not to disturb them, but I still rushed to get over the expanse quickly. Nevertheless, their ghosts seemed to speak to me and say, "We lived in peace, yet this horror happened to us. Don't let it happen again."

The world thought the genocide of the Jews in the second World War could never happen again, but, in fact, it has happened several times since: in Bosnia, in Syria, in Cambodia, and in China, often with more cruelty than than Nazis ever thought of. The realization made me wonder what it is in ordinary people that triggers the ability to act so heinously. Was I capable of killing people indiscriminately? I had been a soldier and fired lethal guns and even a machine gun, but had never been to war. Could I kill someone to protect my country? My family? What made more and more people resort to automatic weapons to wipe out co-workers, fellow students, or people of a different culture or religion?

I had learned the story of the Holocaust growing up, and the world said, "Never again." Yet with seemingly endless wars and mass shootings, the world seemed to be spinning closer and closer to that mindset. I couldn't reconcile it with the seemingly benign world I grew up in. I just hoped some unseen pendulum would swing the world back to a place where children could grow up without fear.

~

On Sunday evening, I got a text message from Ashley: "Anna is in the hospital. She had a headache and joint pain and got very weak." I felt terrible for Anna, but was glad she had decided not to travel with me that weekend.

I called Ashley and told her that Anna had been fine when I left. "Our English neighbor, Ray, went home on holiday, but I'll be back tomorrow."

"Hospitals around there are often more like clinics and only open certain days," Ashley said. "She contacted one of your neighbors, who knew of a hospital about five miles away that had an Australian doctor volunteering there. Apparently they are just keeping her overnight to hydrate her and she'll be home tomorrow. I wanted to see if you would be there."

"Yes, of course. I'll be there in the afternoon," I said, thinking about the six-hour trip.

"Good. Let me know if you need anything. *Kwaheri*!"

About an hour later, I got an email from Anna's mother, Jo. I was surprised because I had never had any contact with her and hadn't even known her name. She was apparently very upset that I had left her sick darling "alone in the middle of Africa." I responded politely that Anna had not been sick when I left, and reminded her that her daughter was twenty-five years old and an experienced traveler. She seemed to have handled the situation well and I would be there soon after she got home.

"It's just so hard being so far away when she needs me," Jo responded. "I appreciate anything you can do."

I sympathized with Anna's mother, since I remembered calls from my son when he was sick with the flu while at University in New York and I was in California. I couldn't do much but offer moral support. I considered how I felt about being blamed for being gone when Anna got sick. Ashley had not said anything explicitly, but seemed surprised I had gone to Rwanda by myself. I had felt some maternal concern about leaving Anna alone, which I was sure she would be horrified to know, since she considered herself fully an adult. But I respected her decision to stay and I was sorry she got sick.

In the past, I might have shouldered the guilt her mother was trying to place on me. Now, I refused to accept the burdens of others. My conscience was clear. I really enjoyed my respite in Rwanda, even the long time spent getting there and back. It had been an adventure, and I felt it would energize me for returning to school.

After another good meal and a last, luxurious, hot shower, I returned to Ngara. Anna was home and feeling a lot better.

"They never did find anything wrong, so it was probably just dehydration," she said.

I helped her finish painting her room, and soon she was sleeping there again. Her new kitten shared her bed, though what help that little mite would be against a rat, I didn't know.

9

WATER, WATER, WHO'S GOT THE WATER?

For every drop of water you waste, you must know that somewhere on Earth, someone is desperately looking for a drop of water.

— MEHMET MURAT ILDAN

We had water in our home for a while after the city engineer made a makeshift repair to the town's water pump, until it finally died for good. Then money had to be raised and a new pump ordered from Dar es Salaam. For months, we begged for water from many sources, managing to get about four fifteen-gallon buckets a week for the both of us. We had to decide whether to use it to drink, wash ourselves, wash our clothes, wash our food, or dump it into the toilet to try to flush it. We didn't always agree.

The toilet tank held about five gallons, so it was easy to

agree that we wouldn't be flushing it more than we had to, usually by pouring a gallon or so quickly into the bowl and hoping it would trigger the flush. Otherwise we ended up with an overflowing toilet bowl with it's unmentionable contents streaming across the floor.

I found that I could go a long time without washing my hair when I wasn't sure where my next drinking water was coming from, but Anna's pride and joy was her long curly red hair. She wanted to wash it three times a week and was willing to live with whatever consequences resulted. If she somehow bargained for some extra water from somewhere, she felt it was only fair that she used it to wash her hair. It led to some arguments.

The teachers who lived behind my school had never had running water, but seemed to have no problem getting regular delivery of buckets of water. I tried to find out how to get this service, but apparently I lived too far out of town.

I asked Mama Rose how she got her water.

"There's a big tank attached to my house," she replied.

"Can I get some?" I asked.

"Oh, I would have to check with my husband. He takes care of all that," she said, looking away from me.

I never heard anything more, and assumed her husband reasonably wanted to keep what they had so he didn't have to worry about finding another water source if the pump problem continued.

"I asked some of the teachers at my school who have water tanks, but they don't want to give me any water because their tanks aren't getting refilled," Anna said.

"Well, the tanks here at Afriline are absolutely empty," I replied. "It's so frustrating. They tell us to wait until they resolve the pump situation or the rainy season comes to fill the tanks. Ashley offered to let us move to alternate housing if it's within the budget, but there really is nowhere to go. And the cost is escalating; it's normally 500 shillings a bucket, but we paid 2,500 for the last one."

"Yes, I remember we bribed that bicycle boy to get our last bucket of water from a local restaurant that has a water tank, but I don't think the owners were happy about it," Anna replied. "Even when we try to be conservative, a bucket only lasts a couple of days."

~

Despite the drama at home, the main topic of conversation at school was graduation. Ngara had the custom of having graduation before final exams for the semester.

"How can people be sure they are graduating if they haven't taken the exams yet?" I asked Melchior, my boss.

"They don't know for sure, but they want to enjoy the party before they find out," he said.

And a party it was. My students weren't graduating, since they were only in their first year of Secondary School, but everyone pitched in to make it a grand party. Students joined committees for clean up, decorations, party favors, food preparation, entertainment, and more. The prospective graduates wore caps and gowns borrowed from the school district and paraded from town to the school, proudly singing a song in Swahili I didn't understand the words to.

I wanted to help in some way and wandered over to where some students and parents were preparing food behind the school. Rice didn't come in small packages, but in large fifty-pound bags. I ended up sifting some and taking out the small stones interspersed with the grains before the students cooked large batches in pots over an open fire. Some parents had donated chickens and a goat, and the smell of meat cooking on skewers made my mouth water. We had bottled water for the ceremony, and I was surprised to see case after case of beer ready for the post-graduation party on campus.

"We voted, and everyone wanted beer to drink," the Principal told me. Apparently there was no restriction against alcohol at school events, at least not this one. And beer was cheaper and more accessible than bottled water. "There will be music and a lot of dancing, also, so be sure to come."

The graduation ceremony was held inside the school meeting hall. The teachers sat at long, decorated tables alongside the front stage, and the students sat in folding chairs facing it. It seemed like every student participated in some kind of performance, whether it was acting in a skit, reciting a poem, demonstrating kickboxing, singing, playing music, or dancing. My students were outstanding, and I felt proud of them.

The downside was that the ceremony took hours, and there was a two-hour intermission before the real party started. I stood outside in the sun talking to one of the teachers, who wanted help understanding the human circulation system. I felt rather tired but, as a nurse, well qualified to talk about the subject.

I was explaining the different chambers of the heart when, all of a sudden, my vision deteriorated into gray blotches, as on a TV set that doesn't have good reception. I tried to concentrate on what I was saying, but got nauseous and apparently passed out in the middle of a sentence. I woke up on the ground to dark faces bending over me, eyes wide so the whites stood out in contrast.

I was taken inside and given some water to drink, then someone called a *piky piky* to take me home. Tanzanian women usually sit modestly sideways on the back of the motorcycle, not touching the driver. I straddled the seat and held on tightly to the driver, too afraid I would fall off to worry about breaking cultural norms. He stayed long enough to watch me stumble into my house. I was glad to be home, but sad that I was missing the graduation party.

I drank some water with about two tablespoons of salt in it. I had never had a problem with dehydration before, and surmised that my diet was deficient in sodium. I grew up near the ocean in California, where the soil had sodium from the salt water that had once covered the land. My diet had always included a fair portion of processed foods, which are also rich in sodium.

In Ngara, my food came almost entirely from the local farmers' markets. As a nurse who had cared for a lot of heart patients, I saw adding salt to food as almost evil, and never got in the habit. Even our peanut butter was purchased from local farmers, who made it with minimal additives and processing. The only packaged things we used were instant coffee, seasonings, and dried milk.

I was probably eating healthier food than I ever had in my life, but the lack of sufficient sodium and water was killing me. I had a large container of salt, but obtaining water continued to be a big issue. Supplies of bottled water in town had dried up. Ray, who worked for a water NGO, had helped us get water but had recently been transferred to the Congo. As time went on, it became more and more difficult to stay hydrated. I cut back further on washing my hair and clothes so that I would have more to drink.

"Please let that water pump be fixed soon," I prayed.

～

Not long after the graduation party we had mid-term break. A short while after that we would have exams and the end of term. The timeline seemed out of whack, but it worked for them. I was tired of the drudgery of feeling deprived of what I considered basic needs, and wanted to get out of town. There was a drought up north in Somalia, but the water problem where we lived was local to Ngara. That left a whole lot of places to go.

"I've been in Africa almost four months and the only wildlife I've seen is two baboons on the side of the road," I complained to Anna one day. That wasn't counting the occasional fist-sized hairy spiders, rats, and lizards in our house. If I stood on our porch, I could see some underfed cows and goats in the distance. The closest we came to wildlife was our adopted ginger and white kitten, Poa, who snuggled contentedly on my lap.

"Sorry, Poa," I said, looking down on him while gently stroking his back. "I know you're doing a great job hunting game around here, but I came to Africa hoping to see your big brothers and sisters."

No response from Poa. He was probably exhausted from chasing that grasshopper around the living room ten minutes before.

"Well, it's almost mid-term break," said Anna, swiping her hand distractedly through her long red curls. "Do you think you could find a safari you can do in a week?"

She taught at a different school and had different time off, so wouldn't be coming with me. I would be traveling across Africa completely on my own. Could I do it? At least Anna would notify the embassy if I didn't return on time.

Our temporary home of Ngara had a single paved road and was definitely not a hotbed of tourist activity. The nearest city was Kigali, the capital of Rwanda, which I had already visited. I decided to return and see if I could book a safari in either Rwanda or neighboring Uganda.

I walked to the dirt field in town known as the "bus station" and found a shared taxi to Rwanda. Experience had taught me that Tanzanian culture is big on sharing. Whenever someone got hurt, sick, married, retired, or any life event, strangers would come to my door with a list of names, looking for a donation, often for people I didn't even know. My king-sized bed would probably be shared by at least four people in a typical Tanzanian household. The sharing culture for taxis often meant that four people shared the front seat, spacious comfort compared with the back of the car, where people were crammed into every nook and cranny. I once saw fourteen people in a Toyota Corolla, a vehicle classified as "compact" in the United States.

I usually rated the front seat. I don't know if it was to honor me as an older person or foreigner or because no one wanted to sit next to me. I inevitably ended up sharing my bucket seat with someone else. Luckily, this time it was a skinny thirteen-year-old girl, so we both had room to stretch our legs.

I opted to stay in a cheaper hotel than on my last visit to Kigali, but I still enjoyed hot running water and good breakfasts. I was ecstatic to have fast and reliable internet access and used it to quickly find a tour provider in Uganda offering a mini safari that I could join on my third day of vacation.

The bus to Kampala, the capital of Uganda and the starting point of my tour, was twenty-four hours each way on 232 miles of mostly unimproved roads. That sounded like a lot of misery and too much time. The flight took less than an hour. I'm all for traveling on a budget, but deciding between $23 for a 24-hour bus ride versus $100 for a 45-minute flight was no contest.

"Yes, come," said a travel agent named Joy, when I called

the travel agency to confirm the safari online date and price. "Your guide will pick you up at the airport."

"Oh, wonderful!" I replied. "I was worried about rushing around a strange African city trying to find your office."

"That's why we have you picked up at the airport," she said. "It's a huge city that grew willy nilly and there aren't many street signs. I think you have to be born here to find anything."

My hotel in Kigali arranged for a driver to pick me up and take me to the airport. I eyed his spotless white shirt, fitted gray suit, blue tie, and neatly trimmed mustache. He held open the rear door of a shiny late-model car. There were no other passengers. After all the ragtag transportation I had used in Tanzania, this felt like the Twilight Zone.

"Are you sure you're here for me?" I asked, astounded to be riding in anything less than ten years old.

"Yes, of course. Mary Morrison," he replied. I felt like a celebrity as I climbed into the back seat and inhaled the scent of new leather. The heady feeling lasted until a policeman stopped us on the way to the airport and began berating my driver in French, the official language of the country. The driver just nodded and pulled out his papers. After more yelling and nodding we were on our way again.

"What was that all about?" I asked, as we continued down the roadway, which was lined with colorful trees and flowers.

"I almost got a ticket because you're not wearing your seatbelt," he explained.

I put my seatbelt on, laughing as I told him about the overstuffed thirty-year-old Toyotas and dirty, T-shirted drivers in Tanzania. The only seat belts I ever saw there were frayed remnants that had long since lost their connectors. He laughed along with me, proud of his shiny, newer car.

After I boarded the small jet, I fell asleep to the drone of the engine and woke up about a half hour later to the overwhelming sight of seemingly endless water that stretched to the horizon. Was that the ocean? I had a moment of panic as I wondered if I'd gotten on the wrong plane. The person next to me confirmed I was looking at Lake Victoria, three times the size of the state of New Jersey and the source of the Nile River. I'd seen it from the ground years before, but a bird's eye view had a totally different impact.

The plane circled down to Entebbe airport, which hugged the shoreline. I was curious to see the site of Operation Thunderbolt, one of the most successful counter-terrorist operations in memory and the subject of several movies. In 1976, a group of Palestinians and Germans hijacked an Air France plane from Athens and threatened to kill all the hostages if fifty-three Palestinian prisoners were not released. Israeli commandos stormed the airport on the same day as the U.S. bicentennial celebration and rescued almost all of the hostages. It was also the day that Benjamin Netanyahu, who later became the Prime Minister of Israel, lost his older brother, one of the commanders of the assault.

Stories of the hijacking and the ignominious Idi Amin, the military dictator who welcomed the hijackers, were about all I then knew about Uganda. I had recently seen *The Last King of Scotland*, a movie about an English doctor who became Idi Amin's personal physician and witnessed firsthand his paranoia and violence. Idi Amin had long since been deposed and died, but I still felt the ghost of his terror-filled regime as I got off the plane.

Feeling numb, I slowly followed the other passengers into the airport terminal and saw a tall, muscular black man wearing khaki pants, a matching multi-pocketed shirt, and a huge smile. He held up a sign with my name on it. "Rescued," I said under my breath as I went to join him.

"Hello, I'm Morris and I will be your guide," he said, as he grabbed my small backpack from my shoulder and transferred it to his own.

"*Hujambo*. I feel a little overwhelmed to be in the place where they had the big raid," I said.

"That was in the old airport next to this one," he replied. "I was a child then. Uganda lost dozens of soldiers and planes, but the planes were mostly Russian and not very good."

I followed him to a Toyota Land Cruiser in the parking lot. I came to know this model well, as it was used on every safari I took in Africa for the next year. I gained a new respect for Toyota after surviving many ventures through mud, rain-swollen rivers, and tire-eating sand.

We drove on a nice, black-topped highway away from the quiet lakeside resort town of Entebbe until we came to the tour office in Kampala, about twenty-five miles away. I met Joy, who gave me a printout of my tour and took my credit card for payment. Eleven hundred dollars seemed like a lot for three nights, but I wasn't too concerned, since other volunteers had told me they spent $600 for one night camping in Serengeti National Park. I felt lucky to have found a tour at all since I signed up at the last minute.

"When will I meet the other people on the tour?" I asked, which elicited a laugh from Joy.

"This is your tour," she said, grinning. "Morris is your driver and you can go wherever you want and stay as long or as little as you want. You just have to show up at the lodges we booked for you."

I was a little flabbergasted. My own tour? My own private car and driver to go when and where I wanted? Not my usual style at all. I am a budget traveler from way back. But I decided to enjoy it, since it was the only African safari tour I could find in my short timeframe. The price was starting to look like a great deal.

"This is Africa," I said to myself. I was more than ready to go find Tarzan's world.

ON SAFARI

No matter how few possessions you own or how little money you have, loving wildlife and nature will make you rich beyond measure.

— PAUL OXTON

---

*M*orris and I drove out of the city in intermittent rain, caught up in the stop-and-go afternoon traffic that comes with being in a city of two million people at rush hour. On one downhill, the brakes didn't catch fast enough and I watched in horror as we slid and then bumped into a boy on rollerblades who was hanging on to the back of the truck in front of us.

"Stay in the car," Morris grunted as he whipped out the door, slamming it after him.

I sat there watching as a crowd gathered around the boy,

who was now lying still in the middle of the road. People in vehicles behind us were honking and yelling. I thought of the stories I had heard of Africans beating up drivers who hit animals, and I wondered how much worse the punishment would be for hitting a person. Would they drag Morris off to jail? It ran through my mind that an African boy who could afford inline skates (the only ones I ever saw in Africa) was probably not a poor farmer's son, but could have influential parents. Would my safari end before I even got out of town?

All of a sudden the boy got up and skated away. Morris got back in our Toyota and started the engine.

"Is he OK?" I asked.

"He's fine," Morris answered, not taking his eyes off the road. "It would have been worse, but a policeman was having tea in that shop on the side of the road and saw what happened. The boy should not have been hanging onto the truck. He thought he could get some money from us if he pretended to be hurt, but when the policeman got there he knew he was in trouble. He got better all of a sudden and left."

I relaxed into my seat and enjoyed watching the scenery as we left the hectic city behind and traveled through the gently rolling hills of the country. After a few hours, we came to a sign at the intersection with a narrow dirt road that said *Chobe Safari Camp – 10 miles.*

Morris had been pointing out interesting things since I met him, but now he got into full safari guide mode and I learned a whole lot more about the natural landscape. Acacia trees were scattered around the mostly flat landscape, and as we came to a thick grove of them he stopped the car in their shade and pointed to the left at two giraffes stretching their necks upward to chomp on the leaves.

"Oh," I cried, enthralled. "Finally, I am seeing some wild animals!"

We watched them for several minutes until Morris pointed to the right. I could see a giraffe's head over another acacia tree in the distance. Suddenly two more heads popped up. I watched the giraffes amble toward us, moving their front and back legs forward on one side and then the other side, unlike most four-legged mammals, who alternate opposite front and back legs. Their necks bobbed up and down as they walked. They looked so ridiculous I had to smile.

I was fascinated, and I was in love. I startled when Morris touched my shoulder and pointed left again. I could see many more giraffe heads bobbing above the trees, and they were coming our way!

Eventually we had about twenty giraffes surrounding us, some only two feet away. We sat silently in the vehicle, looking around at the magnificent creatures that passed us silently. Their long black eyelashes looked like they were coated with several layers of mascara as they blinked against their dark eyes, making me feel like they were winking at me. I felt that they were communicating with me somehow, even in their silence. I felt peace, gentleness, and that a world gone mad had suddenly found its balance in the slow, steady, off-kilter gait of the giraffes.

We sat for about fifteen minutes, until the herd had passed and dusk was upon us. Morris started the engine, and the noise brought me back to reality. But my smile stayed with me. The feeling was so powerful that I knew that whenever I felt down in the future, thinking about those giraffes would put me in a better place.

We continued down the narrow dirt road until the groves of thorny acacia trees suddenly opened up to reveal a massive swath of lawn and beds of colorful flowers. A sprawling low-

LOOKING FOR THE LIONESS

rise building had stone facing that provided a look of permanence, as if it had been part of the landscape for many years.

"Actually, Chobe Safari Lodge just reopened a couple of years ago," said Morris. "Ugandan rebels terrorized this section of the country and used this as their headquarters for many years, completely ruining it. They got kicked to the Congo, on the other side of the river. An Indian family owns the lodge and spent a lot of money refurbishing it."

This was the first time he talked about danger from anything other than wild animals.

"A couple of years ago? Is it safe here now?" I asked.

"There were a lot of rebel factions, but the worst was Joseph Kony's Lord's Resistance Army," Morris explained. "They terrorized Uganda for twenty years and displaced over a million people."

I was horrified to learn that thousands of children were kidnapped to serve in his Army as soldiers or slaves. I consider myself a news junkie, but I felt ashamed that what sounded like a major humanitarian crisis had passed me by, unnoticed or underreported. The military ousted Kony from Uganda in 2006, but when I was there he continued his campaign of terrorism and murder from across the river in the Democratic Republic of the Congo.

"This area was once considered one of the best game parks in Africa," said Morris, now heavily into his guide mode as he tried for a lighter note. "There were a lot of famous visitors, like Winston Churchill and Theodore Roosevelt. Humphrey Bogart and Katharine Hepburn filmed *African Queen* near here."

Morris shared with me that Ernest Hemingway crashed his plane near the base of nearby Murchison Falls in 1954.

"He and his wife weren't hurt, but they were probably scared because they had to camp overnight near the elephants and crocodiles. They waved down a boat the next day and got downriver to a town with an airstrip. After all that, their luck ran out because the rescue plane crashed on takeoff and Hemingway was hurt so badly that he was a wreck for the rest of his life."

Hemingway was a famous adventurer and probably made of tough stuff. I pictured myself in his situation, shaken by near-death in a plane crash, trying to sleep by the river with no equipment or food, listening to a horde of mosquitoes and unseen animals foraging on the shore. And then crashing again the next day, in the rescue plane. All I felt was sheer panic. I tried to relax as I listened to the soft tones of Morris continuing his history lesson.

He told me that, at the time of independence from Britain in 1962, the area had large populations of all of the Big Five, a game hunter's holy grail: elephants, lions, leopards, water buffaloes, and rhinos. Several regime changes and military takeovers plagued the nation for years, leading to an end of conservation measures and a takeover of the area by rebels and poachers. Idi Amin, Uganda's infamous dictator, closed the country to foreign visitors in 1972.

"I remember trying to get into Uganda with a tour group the first time I came to Africa in 1975," I told Morris. "Idi Amin still wasn't letting anyone in, but he had personally wined and dined a tour group three weeks before us, so we took a chance. We crossed the border from Zaire and the Ugandan border officials wouldn't let us in. In the meantime, the Zaire border had closed while our tour guide was arguing with the Ugandans. We were stuck in 'no man's land' since we couldn't go forward or backward."

"What did you do?" asked Morris.

"It was Christmas, and we had big plans for a celebration. I was twenty-one years old and felt devastated that we would have a terrible Christmas. The older and wiser people in the group stayed cheerful and made it an adventure. Camping in 'no man's land' ended up being one of my most memorable Christmases. It was a big lesson for me that I should have learned earlier. If you're with the right people, not much else matters."

"Yes," Morris laughed. "In English, you say, 'When you get lemons, make lemonade.'"

I reflected on the truth of what Morris said, and how I had felt when that potentially disastrous Christmas turned magical when a few people turned everyone's mood around. I had thought my ex-husband was "the right person," but for years glimpses of magic were rare. I internalized it as my fault for not being pretty enough, thin enough, smart enough, outgoing enough, and an ongoing litany of negative thinking, all of which probably made me a depressing person to be around. If I got negative vibes from friends or family, I just saw them less often or extricated myself entirely from the relationships. It was harder to do that in a marriage, when you had pledged "till death do us part." My husband might have been the right person for me twenty-five years before, but we had both changed and weren't "right" any longer.

It was past time to put the past in the past. I had to banish the negativity that had been crushing me for decades and find a positive environment with a new tribe of "right" people who would bring out the best in me.

Morris interrupted my reflections by continuing in guide mode. "The military and the rebels killed most of the game around here as they scavenged for food. There wasn't really anybody watching, so poachers felt free to kill animals for their tusks and horns. The Chinese were paying a fortune for them. There were over 14,000 elephants here in the 1960s but only 250 by 1990. Rhinos were totally wiped out."

"Is there anything left for me to see?" I gasped, disappointed that the giraffes might be the high point of my trip. Hearing about the devastating loss of wild animals left me feeling incredibly sad. What would the world be like if all the animal stories we grew up with were just fantasies about creatures gone the way of the dinosaurs? Most people might never see a lion, a giraffe, or an elephant, but just knowing it was possible made those stories real. All the better if they could be seen in their natural habitat, and not just in zoos.

"Yes," Morris laughed. "You will see lots of animals. We made lemonade."

I felt reassured as we checked into the lodge. Morris went off to visit with his fellow guides and I wandered outside to the large terrace overlooking the huge swimming pool. I gazed beyond it at a long stretch of the Victoria Nile River, crashing noisily around boulders in its path. The Nile River had so many historical associations for me that my mind careened between thoughts of Pharaohs, tombs, Alexander the Great, Cleopatra, Julius Caesar, and Napoleon. We were a long way from Cairo, but I still felt amazed to be standing where great explorers had possibly stood, filled with determination to find the source of the great river.

I met Ted, a long, tall Texan, while having a glass of wine on the terrace. The only wine I ever found in Ngara was altar wine, so I was enjoying the ambience and invited him to join me.

I suspect most Americans come to Africa to see wild animals. Ted was there for oil. "All of the oil in Uganda is imported, but a few years ago they discovered over a billion gallons of commercially viable oil near Murchison Falls," he said. "Right now, most people here depend on charcoal and wood for energy, along with some hydropower from dams built in the 1980s."

We sat back and enjoyed the cool evening breeze. "Uganda is taking this very slowly." Ted explained, as he snuggled deeper into his big rattan chair. "They have seen what Big Oil has done to other countries and want to make sure the Ugandan people get the most benefit from it, not foreign corporations. They need help, but they want to avoid corruption and environmental damage as much as they can. I'm a consultant for an environmental waste management company they are working with, and I can tell they are serious about getting this right."

Dusk quickly turned to night as we sat on the terrace sipping our wine. As I contemplated an African government that was actively trying to avoid the legacy of corruption that had ruined so many fledgling African nations after independence, I noticed some large black shapes emerging slowly from the river and ambling toward the floodlights that dotted the landscape. Eventually, I could make out hippos grazing serenely on the grass.

"They come right up into the parking lot," our waiter warned, as he passed by and noticed our attention to the animals below. "Be careful when you go to your rooms. They can be dangerous." I had already read that hippos killed more people than any other animal in Africa. They don't eat meat but apparently have bad tempers, are deceptively quicker than they look, and have enormous jaws and tusks that can inflict fatal wounds.

"That feels like a cue for me to say goodnight," I told Ted. For safety's sake, I skipped the shortcut down the outside stairs and went back through the lobby to my ground floor room. I sat outside on the concrete patio facing the river for a while in the cool darkness, but no hippos came calling. I had to be up early for my game drive, so I closed the mosquito net around my bed and fell into a welcome sleep.

Morning found me back on the terrace overlooking the Nile River, enjoying breakfast while watching the hippos and water buffalo. Morris came to collect me for our game drive. The direct route to the sister lodge at Paraa was a one-hour drive, but we took a circuitous route for five hours through several different ecosystems.

Thick acacia forest turned into savannah with clusters of fig trees, then drier savannah with Borassa palm trees. Lastly, we passed through rainforest along the Albert Nile. I saw an abundance of hartebeests, Uganda koes, baboons, warthogs, and giraffes. There were lesser amounts of bushbucks, vervet monkeys, and elephants. Each sighting seemed to make my heart beat faster, as I watched the animals in awe.

"You did make lemonade," I joked, as Morris raised the top of the Toyota so I could stand up and take pictures in all directions while enjoying the sun and the fresh breeze. He was down in the cab driving and I saw no other vehicles or people. I felt like I was in a mobile cocoon, with the whole of Murchison Falls National Park to myself.

At one point he stopped about ten feet from some Cape buffalo, making sure we stayed downwind and warning me to be very quiet.

"They can't see very well but they will charge if they know we are here," he said. I took him seriously as some of those bulls weighed a ton and would win any confrontation with us. They gored and killed many people every year, unlike the relatively placid Asian water buffaloes.

Later, we saw another safari vehicle stopped near a thicket. Morris asked the guide in the other car what they were looking at.

"A female lion," he said, "but she's hiding in there and hasn't moved."

I focused all my mental energies on the lioness, hoping

my telepathic vibes would get the animal to show herself. The brambles she was hiding in made it so dark I could barely distinguish her. I saw her ears flick and her head move slightly before she grew still again. It was disappointing to think that this obscure view might be the only lion I would see in the wild on this trip. It just drove home the fact that no matter how much money you pay for the privilege of communing with her, Nature has her own path.

As we continued driving across the savannah, I contemplated the kinship I felt with that lioness. I used to think of myself as an adventurer, independent, and a little fierce in my own way. The decades before coming back to Africa had gradually surrounded me with brambles that closed in tighter and tighter, until they seemed to be suffocating me. I was not even aware of how stifling the bindings were until I broke free and came to Africa, leaving behind most of the responsibilities and commitments to work, community, and family I had gradually piled on myself over the years.

After what felt like a long period of stagnation, living to satisfy external demands, I was finally free to find happiness for my own sake. I wasn't sure what would make me happy, but I reveled in the freedom to find out.

After the game drive, we checked into the Paraa Safari Lodge, downriver from Chobe Lodge. This hotel had also been severely damaged by rebels. The new decor was "early African explorer," with the closet doors made to look like old steamer trunks and decorative touches like old metal typewriters and antique navigational tools. The public rooms were named for Victorian-era African explorers like David Livingstone and John Speke, and decorated accordingly.

In the afternoon, Morris dropped me off at the river dock so I could board the *African Queen*, a bi-level pontoon boat, for a three-hour excursion to Murchison Falls and back. My fifteen fellow travelers included a Norwegian, an Englishman, several Swiss and Ugandan tourists, and a black American rock band from New York that had been performing in Kampala.

As we progressed slowly upriver, I scanned the depths of jungle all around me for any sound or movement. Fish eagles soared overhead while complacent white herons and egrets stood sentinel in the marshes. Groups of hippos were submerged in the water with only their protuberant eyes and wiggly ears showing. A few fed on the shore, their huge bodies showing large, ugly red patches that the river guide told us were from sunburn. Unlike humans, they don't generate new skin following a burn and can die without its protection. Crocodiles were either motionless, resembling logs you could sit on, or slithering along the shore and into the water. I reveled in the beauty and peace of it all, but I was glad I was drifting by in the boat. As much as I enjoyed watching the hippos and crocodiles, I didn't want to swim with them.

The next morning's drive to the top of Murchison Falls was all on unpaved road. After about two hours, we turned onto a much rougher and narrower dirt road and drove for a few miles to an unimproved parking lot with a small, weathered sign pointing to Murchison Falls. A safari vehicle exited as we arrived, leaving ours the lone vehicle in the lot. The Falls had seemed unimpressive from the boat, so I was really surprised when Morris guided me down the overgrown trail to look down and see one of nature's more violent manifestations.

Imagine the wide Nile River with Class V rapids forced through a 23-foot-wide gorge, surrounded by huge boulders the size of buildings and high jungle-covered walls all around. The extreme water pressure generated an immense amount of spray. I clambered over rocks to get near the river and stood alone between two huge rainbows. I stayed there for a while and enjoyed feeling the sun warm me as the cold river spray gave me chills and the thundering water boomed in my ears.

As I stood there, I felt the essence of Africa: dangerous beauty, peace, and violence coexisting in an awesome mix that wrenched my heart. It felt like an incubator for the soul that organically gathered energy from my rooted feet and caused me to throw my hands up in the air and yell, "I'm really here! This is Africa!"

I drew the feeling deep into my mind and heart, knowing it was something rare and special.

~

My final lesson in regeneration on that trip happened at Ziwa Rhino Sanctuary. An exhibit in the Visitors Center lamented the extinction of the hundreds of both black and white rhinos that used to roam Uganda. As Morris had mentioned, the rhinos were decimated as poachers tried to meet the demands of Asians who considered the horns an aphrodisiac. In the spirit of making lemonade, a campaign started to bring the rhinos back. A ranch donated a thirty-year lease of land for a sanctuary and the U.S. Wildlife Federation gave a grant to get it started. Kenya donated four rhinos in 2005.

The next year, two rhinos from Walt Disney Animal Kingdom in Florida returned to their genealogical homeland with the noble purpose of forming the nucleus of the rebirth of the rhino population in Uganda. The American female and one of the Kenyan males had a baby in 2009, appropriately named Obama. The next baby was called Malia after President Obama's oldest daughter.

The gamekeeper took a group of us tourists out, urging that we walk single file and not make any noise. Of course, he knew right where the rhinos were, since they keep constant tabs on them. He told us they are nocturnal and mostly sleep during the day. Sure enough, we came upon a group of rhinos resting peacefully in dense bush under some trees. The game-keeper identified Obama and Malia for us and told us to be very quiet so we didn't disturb them. It wasn't an exciting encounter, but I felt better knowing that people cared about the animals and were doing something for them. The preserve's priority was the animals, and the tourists were just a way of raising funds.

When I visited in 2011, they had ten rhinos. As of 2018, they had twenty-two. When the population reaches thirty, they will start introducing them into the wild. A high electric fence and around-the-clock patrols by gamekeepers and armed guards showed the seriousness of the endeavor. The word was out that suspected poachers would be shot first and questioned later.

During my time in Africa, I saw and heard of many of these "regeneration" projects to encourage biodiversity and repopulate the seriously declining populations of wild animals in Africa. Many projects have been vilified for training the animals to interact with people for glorified "tourist traps," whose main goal is to make money for the owners. This interaction makes the animals unafraid of humans and unsuitable to ever return to the wild.

For serious ventures with positive reported gains, like the rhino sanctuary, it seems like a losing battle against the forces of climate change, loss of habitat, human encroachment, and greed. I think about how long those rhinos will last once they start releasing them. Sadly, history tells me it won't be long.

Back in Kampala, I said goodbye to Morris. After only three days together, he felt like a friend.

"Thank you so much for sharing part of your country with me," I said. "It felt like our own private game park, since you knew where to go to avoid other tourists. I feel honored to have been up close with so many different animals in their natural habitat. I'm sure it wouldn't have been the same without you."

"*Asante sana*," replied Morris, slipping into the Swahili that had been banned under Idi Amin as a tool of the *msungus*. "You feel a bond with the animals here, so I know you will come back someday."

I nodded, liking the sentiment but thinking it was unlikely that, once I got home to "real" life, I would ever be able to come back. I had seen a lot of the world, but, in that moment, the world of my mind was still small.

I stayed in a hotel overnight, where I was able to access the U.S. State Department website on the hotel internet before catching a flight back to Rwanda. I was reassured that the Murchison Falls area was now clear of rebel activity and safe for tourists.

A week later I read a newspaper article that said that President Obama was sending one hundred combat troops to help capture Joseph Kony and his officers in the area of the Congo, Uganda, and the Central African Republic.

Although I had left the area by then, I still felt a shiver down my back. So much blood, both human and animal, had been shed on the ground I had recently walked.

TIA.

11

CELEBRATION

When traveling in rural Africa, it is important to not actually "go" to the hospital until the patient is on the brink of expiration. Otherwise, things are going to get worse.

— JOSH GATES, *DESTINATION TRUTH*

*M*y safari to Uganda felt like a dream as I returned to school the following week. I had struggled in the still unfamiliar role of teacher for a couple of hundred high school students. End-of-semester exams would soon be upon us, and they would show how effective my teaching had been. I thought I had kept the students' attention by roaming the room as I talked, making eye contact, and wordlessly pointing to the desks of students who were working on other things as I passed by. That had never worked very well with my own son, but it seemed to be enough for these students to put away whatever they were doing and focus on me.

"Teaching seems a lot easier now that I have things figured out and have a rhythm," I told Melchior, as we discussed the final exam schedule for the semester. I had to formulate thirty questions and submit them to the secretary so that she could type them up and make copies of the exam.

At this point in the semester, my two hundred students had dwindled by about a third due to nonpayment of fees, illness, and other reasons I hadn't been told about. I'm ashamed to say I still had not learned all their names. I was pretty good about who was in the same family, but names were hard. The Muslim boys were mostly Mohamed, Moshid, and Mustafa. The Christians all had Biblical names, which I thought would be easier to remember. But then I learned that the English names had mostly been given to them in school. Most of the students also had African names, and they answered to both, which made it even more confusing.

I didn't know if it was unusual for a teacher to not know the names of her students. Anna seemed to know all of hers, but I was embarrassed to ask her if that was true. My own past teachers had always known mine, at least I think they did, but they could have been cheating by referring to the seating charts they kept on their desks. I wondered if age was affecting my memory, or if I was just a bad teacher. Surely good teachers knew their students' names?

Taking roll call at the start of class used to help me to learn names. But now I didn't have that task because every class had a "head girl" or "head boy," the student in that stream selected to take roll and do other administrative chores in each class. Supposedly, this taught them to be responsible and freed up the teacher to use the time to actually teach, but I would have felt more effective if I had gotten to know the students a little better. A name is important to the person that holds it, and I felt that I had let some of them down by not learning this basic information about them.

One of my students left school because she got pregnant. Investigation revealed that one of the temporary teachers had demanded sex in return for a better grade. Ashley had warned us this happened in Tanzania, but I was shocked that it happened to people I knew. Apparently Mama Caritas had stepped in, and both were gone before I knew about it. Financial and family expectations put immense pressure on students to succeed, especially the girls. If graduation didn't get them a career, it would at least get them a better husband.

I had no idea what would happen to this girl now, and nobody seemed to want to talk about it. At least they wouldn't talk about it with me, which made me feel like the *mzungu* outsider. I told myself they just didn't want to voice the shame that this happened at their school.

Three of my students left because of AIDS. It was a mandated subject in my curriculum, as it is in every grade from primary school on up. I made sure to spend a whole class on it. The first thing I asked was, "Raise your hand if you know anyone who has HIV or AIDS."

At the time, the government said the rate was about eight percent of the population, including "half the bar and restaurant workers in Dar." I was living in a rural area on the opposite side of the country, so I was surprised to see that almost every hand went up. Further questioning found that about half had a relative with AIDS, and the rest knew people who had it. Many of the orphans had lost one or both parents to the disease.

I realized that this might be the most important class I taught all semester. I gave them the medical and statistical information I had gathered. I brought a cartoon book I found in the school library, which told the story of a girl who dated a guy with a flashy car and lots of money, which was fun until he left her pregnant and infected with HIV while he went on to the next girl. We discussed dating and students shared their experiences. It was the most open and free-flowing discussion we had all semester.

The girls, especially, seemed determined to stay in school, even if it meant not dating until they finished. The boys seemed more afraid of getting sick and dying. I hate to use fear as an educational tool, but in this case, I hoped it made an impact.

~

I really wanted my students to succeed with their exams, so the two classes before the test were spent reviewing the material we had covered, especially the parts I had based my questions on. I wanted to give a reward to encourage them to show up for the review, so I bought three packs of fifty pens for ten dollars each and promised a pen to any student who showed up. Only a few people missed one or both days.

I was sympathetic when one of my "head girls" came to me and said she lost her pen and could she please have another one. "Head" students are picked because they are thought to be responsible and trustworthy, so I readily complied. By the end of that day, I had four other students, all of whom I considered as some of my best, tell me they lost their pens. It struck me that this might be a scam to get more free pens.

I was a little disappointed that the students might be lying to me and I didn't want to reward that behavior, but I had extra pens so I gave them the benefit of the doubt. If I was going to give them away, I felt better giving them to students who I thought would make use of them. Also, they were all girls, and I felt good giving them even a slight advantage in a patriarchal society where girls had a lot of disadvantages.

The day before the exams, we had a school meeting with the parents of students who expected to continue on. The teachers sat on chairs lined up in two rows on the stage, while the parents and some students sat in rows of chairs below. The principal stood and congratulated the students who had come that far and wished them luck on their exams.

"But it's very important that we get at least half of the school fees for the next semester by the end of next week, or they won't be able to attend until that is paid," he said. He then went on to list some recent student and school achievements before saying, "Now I want to introduce you to our volunteer teacher from America."

He pointed to me proudly, like I was a prize and made the school fees worthwhile. I was surprised he even mentioned me. Mama Rose, sitting beside me, gave me a small shove on the shoulder and said, "Get up! They want to hear from you."

The Principal gestured at me to come and stand next to him, while the parents clapped politely. "Mama Mary has spent her own money to make sure all the students had pens before the exams," he continued.

I don't know how he knew about that and don't remember what I said in the short speech I gave, but I felt embarrassed to be recognized for such a small thing, knowing how these people sacrificed to keep their children in school. I was more shocked when the parents gave me a standing ovation. I nodded, sure my face was beet red, and sat back down. I was thankful the meeting was soon over.

Exams were scheduled over four days, with my four streams completed in the first two days. I had tried to make the questions fairly easy and made sure I covered them thoroughly in the review, even to the point of giving hints like, "You may want to remember this part," or "This is important," as I remembered teachers had once done for me. Still, I was worried that I hadn't made the questions clear enough, or that the students would misunderstand them. I didn't want to be the reason they didn't finish school.

I was pleasantly surprised when almost all my students passed my test. There was only one boy that missed over half the questions, but I didn't feel guilty because he had missed a lot of classes and had not attended either of the review classes. I was only a little perturbed that almost all of my students got better grades in math and physics. Were the teachers better? Were my questions harder? Is it because I couldn't explain in Swahili? Did the students just like those subjects more?

I had no answers. I just hoped I was giving more help than harm. I reached for the positive: almost all of my students had passed. I let the other questions go and decided to concentrate my energy on the coming days off. I had been so focused on the exams that I hadn't made any plans for my one-week vacation before the students returned to get their test results.

～

But first, there was a party to attend. The people of Tanzania love parties, and the fiftieth anniversary of independence from the colonial powers gave them a big reason to celebrate. There was a *shirehe* (festival) in a field near downtown. Booths with food, games, health education, and crafts clustered around a central area, and a temporary stage was built at one end. Concern (the water NGO) and Womencraft (a local basket-making NGO) both had booths at the festival. My students had all been released from school that morning to sing on the stage. I arrived too late for that, but many students and teachers were still there in the afternoon and greeted me as Anna and I wandered from booth to booth.

I was walking across the field when I suddenly got the symptoms I now recognized as dehydration: nausea, dizziness, and blurred vision. I was probably seconds away from passing out when I reached forward to hit Anna in the back and told her I was going to faint. She almost immediately found a plastic chair for me to sit on and pushed my head down between my knees.

I couldn't believe this was happening to me again, and that it came on so suddenly, with almost no warning. I gratefully accepted a bottle of water someone thrust at me. Anna found one of her teachers to give me a ride home, but he was going somewhere else first and would come back "in fifteen minutes" to get me. Not trusting this, I told Anna to find me a *picky picky* so I could go home right away. Thankfully, it was not a long way. At home, I drank a lot of water and laid down.

The next day, Saturday, I felt better but not quite up to going to a birthday party we were invited to at Garden Pause. Beer would be the main sustenance at the party, and I sure didn't need anything to further deplete my fluids.

I expected to feel better the following day, but I got out of bed that morning and immediately fell on the concrete floor. I did not lose consciousness, but suddenly the floor was just there. Unhurt, I managed to crawl back into bed and was assaulted by vertigo. The room was spinning even with my eyes closed.

By this time I was frightened. I drank more water and eventually went back to sleep, which seemed the safest option. When I got up again, I sat on the side of the bed for a full minute before standing and immediately reached for the wall opposite my bed for support. I was determined not to fall down again.

I slowly left the room, holding on to the walls in what I think of as "the Marge walk" after seeing my mother-in-law do this many times in the past. Why had we ever joked about this? She was at that moment in the last stages of terminal cancer, and would be dead by the end of the year. She had been a true friend, and I felt terrible remorse that I was not there for her at the end, even though we had known it would happen that way when we said our final goodbyes months earlier. At the same time, I was going through a lot of life changes and was probably not the best person to show her a happy face. I had to figure out who I had become and who I aspired to be before I could be a true friend. But first, I had to get out of Africa alive.

I almost called Anna take me to the hospital, but dizziness improved after I drank some water with about three table-spoons of salt in it. I had read that people hiking in the Grand Canyon in Arizona have problems because they drink plain water when they needed electrolytes, like sodium and potassium. Additional water just compounds the problem by washing more electrolytes out of their bodies. I could not walk on my own at this point, and decided to go to bed and see how I felt the next day.

Unfortunately the saline water gave me diarrhea, which persisted all night until I took some Pepto Bismol the next day. Diarrhea is not a good thing when you're already dehydrated and don't have enough water on hand to flush the toilet. Also, I was not eating much, since there was no electricity for cooking and little food in the house, not even bread or crackers. Anna still had exams to give and was away at school most of the day.

On Monday, I felt a little better. I texted the Australian doctor who worked occasionally at the Diocese hospital in Murgwanza and asked her if I should go there or the government hospital, which was closer to where I lived. She was homeschooling her children that day and would not be there, but suggested I go to Murgwanza because the laboratory was better.

I called a *picky picky* to take me to the hospital. The driver, Justin, helped me with registration and told me where to sit. I was glad to have his help, since all the signs were in Swahili. The hospital was a one-story building of offices built around an open central area. There were three windows opposite the front door: Registration, Medical Records, and Payment. Patients sat on benches in the open air central area and along the walls and waited to be called. After about twenty minutes, I was called to see a nurse. She took my blood pressure, which was fine, and ordered blood tests for malaria and anemia and a stool test for parasites.

"I think I'm dehydrated. I almost passed out yesterday and now I can barely walk. Can you please check my electrolytes?" I wanted to know if my sodium and potassium were depleted or unbalanced, which I knew could be serious and even fatal.

"We can't do that," she told me.

"Why not?" I questioned.

She checked with her superior and still came back with a definite no, but no further explanation. I was shown to another outbuilding, which housed the laboratory, and my finger was pricked for blood tests for malaria and hemoglobin. After going back to the main building to wait for another half hour, I got my test results, which were negative for malaria. My hemoglobin was a little low, especially since I was taking an iron supplement.

I got a prescription for electrolyte salts and waited at another building about forty-five minutes to get this filled. After twenty-four hours of diarrhea, I was unable to give a stool specimen. I took the bottle home and returned it with a specimen the next day. Anna had recently been treated for parasites, and I wanted to be tested to make sure this was not contributing to my poor health status. Happily, it was negative.

My total bill was 3,000 shillings for registration (about two dollars) and 600 shillings (forty cents) for six packets of electrolyte salts. I was at the hospital about three hours the first day and one hour on the second day. I did not see a doctor until the second day, and he told me they would do a blood test for parasites if I still had dizziness after three more days. I was told to eat a lot of fruit.

"Why wouldn't they do an electrolyte test?" I asked the doctor.

"It's not cost effective," he said. "The test would have to go to Mwanza. If the results aren't good, by the time we get them back it would be too late to do anything anyway, so we don't bother."

The treatment was basic but effective. The minimal diagnostic testing was very different than in the U.S., where they would do multiple tests to rule out everything under the sun. I would have felt better if they had done basic blood tests (i.e., complete blood count and metabolic panel). I felt better, but not one hundred percent, so I just hoped I was okay. I had no desire to be seriously ill, especially in Africa.

I almost laughed when I got an email from a friend in California a few weeks later: "I got dizzy a few times. They admitted me to the hospital with dehydration and I stayed a couple of days to get IVs. They said I could have died." I suspected my condition had been more serious than hers, but that her bill was a heck of a lot more.

~

The day after I saw the doctor, I noticed swarms of grasshoppers jumping all around the compound. They were about three to four inches long and bright green. The cleaning lady at the compound asked me for a jar so that she could catch some and take them home. I didn't realize she meant to eat them until Anna told me that all the teachers and students at her school were outside catching them to fry in oil for a snack. She brought some home for me to taste. I was a little leery because I had recently been sick, but they were apparently considered a treat and I wanted to try them. The wings and legs had been removed and the bodies fried in butter and salt.

"I think anything fried in butter tastes like a good snack food," said Anna.

"You're right," I agreed. "But that doesn't mean I want to cook some more. I killed a couple that got in our house and was glad that Poa came home and ate them so I didn't have to pick them up. He must like them, too. He's been staying outside more because he loves to stalk things."

"I'm glad there's plenty of food out there for him to eat," said Anna. "I want him to be independent so I can go away for a day and not worry about him." A veterinarian who lived in the compound had given him a rabies shot, so we were hopeful he wouldn't bring any diseases home with him.

The grasshoppers were the first of a "wave of locusts" that soon was so dense it covered the sun, as well as the ground. They were thick on the thatched roofs and some invaded our house. Poa saw the infiltration as more of a game and enjoyed chasing the few that got in around the house. Anna and I did not take the opportunity to tap into the free source of protein. Luckily, the local harvest was over and the swarm soon moved on, seeking better feeding grounds.

~

Thursday was my birthday and also the American Thanksgiving holiday. I gave out my final exam results that day so I was finished with school for the semester. Anna was still going because she was Teacher on Duty for the week, something I was never called to do. Since she refused to punish students, she mainly sat around and took care of any issues that came up.

When Anna finally got home, she related an incident concerning two of her best Form 2 students who had not shown up for one of their final exams. They told Anna they wore athletic shoes to school because their black shoes had gotten all wet. The Vice Principal told them to go home because they were not in uniform. They didn't have other clean shoes at home so they borrowed shoes from other students to wear for the exam. Somehow, this was discovered before the test and the word was out that everyone involved was going to get punished. Anna was worried because, from what she had witnessed, punishment at that school ranged from a slap on the hand with a stick to getting severely beaten up.

"I was able to talk the teachers into not punishing the students, but the students had no way of knowing this and continued to hide so they wouldn't get punished. When the exam took place, they were still hiding. Final exams can't be made up, so they can't go on to Form 3.

"These are bright, articulate kids from single-parent

143

farmer families," lamented Anna. "I know they work hard because I have tutored them. They also work after school and on weekends to help pay school fees. Their lives are seriously damaged because they wore the wrong shoes to school!"

"TIA," I whispered to myself, not wanting to upset her more.

Anna made us a healthy Thanksgiving dinner of scrambled eggs, rice, cooked spinach, sliced tomatoes, and toast. It sounds humble, but it was a feast for us and was the best and healthiest meal I had had in a long time.

I was so grateful to be able to eat it and keep it down that I didn't miss the usual turkey dinner one bit.

12

LEAVING NGARA

She is a lioness. Let her believe in herself!

— AVIJEET DAS

---

*A*s the months passed, home life in Ngara continued to go downhill, with ongoing water, power, and sewage problems. Our lovely hot water shower had been installed for weeks, but we had never been able to use it because we lacked running water. We were only able to get a couple of fifteen-gallon buckets of water about twice a week.

The compound management moved us to a new house when they couldn't fix the septic line in our old one. For two weeks, sewage had been backing up into the shower pan every time we flushed the toilet, which we only did a few days a week due to lack of water. The smell had gotten pretty bad. The new house was an improvement because the septic line ran downhill, so would be less likely to back up. Anna insisted toilet paper should go in the trash instead of the toilet

145

so we wouldn't have a repeat of the problem. I agreed, since this was standard practice in many countries I had visited that had poor plumbing. The new house was a little bigger, with a separate kitchen and lots of cabinets. We had our same double hotplate but still no running water.

The United Nations definition of absolute poverty is not having adequate food, safe drinking water, sanitation facilities, health, shelter, education, and information.

"We're more than halfway there," I joked to Anna, but it wasn't really funny. I became dizzy and fell down a few more times after that due to continued dehydration. Toward the end, I was going to Rwanda almost every weekend. Although I found cheaper places to stay, Rwanda always made me feel like I was in the lap of luxury, with fabulous food and all the hot showers I wanted. Kigali had become my refugee camp.

I was contracted to teach another semester, but at this point, I felt that my health was threatened. I loved my students, mostly bright, eager children who seemed to like my classes, maybe because I didn't beat them like many of the African teachers did. The school didn't have running water and electricity could only be accessed in the office. I doubted if most of the students had either in their homes. They were born to the country and had the support and know-how of their large extended families. I had neither.

"My health keeps going downhill, so I might as well just leave," I told Mama Caritas.

She gave me a sad smile. "You're not African." I felt the chasm between us. I was from the supposedly superior society, there to pass on my knowledge to the less fortunate, but I had never felt so weak and incapable. I lamented that I was in no condition to give my students the teacher they deserved. I wanted to show them a bright, positive role model, but I felt like I was barely hanging on.

Anna was not feeling the effects of our living situation as much as I was and elected to stay and fulfill her contract. She had started applying for NGO jobs and thought it would look bad on her resume if she left early. I had just hit the official Tanzanian teacher retirement age, so I had no such qualms.

Due to our limited seating, I wrote invitations to a going-away party to only three of my fellow teachers. To my surprise, eight teachers showed up, along with the Principal, the school secretary, and Mama Caritas. Anna had volunteered in soup kitchens in New York City and was prepared with huge batches of coconut rice and cabbage salad. I sliced up pineapples for dessert. The Afriline Canteen supplied beer and soda. It all worked out, as we were able to borrow some chairs from neighbors and people took turns standing up.

Some lovely speeches were given that made me cry. Anna gave me a woolen shawl as a going-away present. The teachers gave me two *kangas,* bright, dark yellow lengths of cloth in African designs.

"Gold is a color for good luck, and also for goodbye," explained Mama Rose as she put her arm around my shoulders. "We wish you a safe journey."

I was so full of emotion that I almost wanted to stay, but I knew there was no turning back. There was no telling when the water and electricity would return, and more importantly, I needed to restore my health. I still had no home to return to, since my renter had five more months on his contract. I planned no further ahead than a week at a resort in Victoria Falls, Zimbabwe, which, decades before, had been a happy place for me when I was at another crossroad in my life.

From there, I would see where life would take me. I was hopeful that I would recover and go on to a new adventure, either in Africa, or somewhere else. Going home was a possibility, but not my preferred option. I was afraid of getting sucked into the same toxic patterns that had made my life miserable in the first place.

A little heartsick, I faced the daunting task of packing up all my belongings, which had grown after living in Tanzania for six months. Even though it was cheaper, I knew it would be difficult to transport everything with a shared taxi, especially in my weakened state. Besides having less security for belongings, I would have to wait in Ngara and at the transfer point in Benako until the taxi had at least six passengers. This could take up to an hour at each point. I opted to splurge on a taxi to pick me up and take me all the way to the border. The long way on tarmac road cost 45,000 shillings (thirty dollars), and the short way on dirt road cost 30,000 (twenty dollars). I went for cheap, because I didn't mind a few bumps as long as it wasn't my car.

Sammy, the taxi driver, picked me up at our house and took me straight to the river border at Rusumo on a dirt road through villages and fields. The bridge over the river was out, so we unexpectedly had to take a car ferry.

"Are you still going to make a profit on this?" I asked, as I watched him shell out the unexpected cost of the ferry. He had already lost a lot of time when we had to stop to change a tire.

"No worries," he laughed. "My family will eat tonight."

The ferry ride took about two minutes. Instead of just dumping me at the border, Sammy waited in the car with my luggage until I got through Tanzania immigration. I was a little leery of leaving everything I owned in a car with a stranger who could just drive off, no matter how nice he seemed, but both the Tanzania and Rwanda immigration offices were up steep stairs and usually had lines of people waiting. It was not too bad with a daypack, but hefting a large duffle bag would have been a problem. After I finished in

Tanzania, he drove me past the rushing waterfall that seemed to make a mockery of my dehydrated state and down the long hill to the Rwanda immigration office. He stayed in the car with my luggage on the Tanzania side until I was cleared by immigration, then arranged for someone to carry my luggage to the Kigali-bound minibus.

"I can't imagine doing this without you," I said, as I paid him and added a big tip. "You really helped me a lot." Just walking up and down all the stairs had exhausted me. It would have been ten times worse with the duffle bag and walking the half mile between border stations instead of riding in the car.

"*Asante sana,* Mama Mary," he replied. "My niece is one of your students and spoke of your kindness and caring. We are so glad you spent time with us in Ngara."

Just another example that what goes around, comes around.

I was able to change my remaining Tanzanian money into Rwandan francs, but I still had limited cash. I had to pay cash for two seats on the bus, since they required I purchase an extra seat for my duffel bag. My American dollars were long gone. Rwanda money is not recognized as an international currency, so I couldn't use my ATM card there. Being rich in credit but poor in actual cash won't buy dinner if nobody accepts your credit.

I stayed at a nicer hotel in Kigali that I knew would take my credit card for food and lodging. They also gave me a free ride to the airport, so I was happy to have thirty dollars worth of extra Rwanda money that had been budgeted for that. The bad thing was that nobody would change it at the airport when I landed in South Africa, so the Rwanda francs were useless and I had no other currency to exchange. It's bad enough to feel weak and unhealthy;

poverty on top of that was just too much. Fortunately, South African rands are internationally accepted, so I was able to use the ATM to get some money for the next leg of my trip.

~

I usually don't return to places I have previously traveled to, preferring to see something new, but Victoria Falls in Zimbabwe was one of my favorite places I had ever been to and I longed for the peaceful, healing energy I had felt there thirty five years before.

My body felt severely depleted after living in Ngara. I estimate I had lost at least thirty pounds, because I had to purchase a belt to manage the several inch gap at the waist of my once snug pants to keep them from sliding off. That wasn't just from poor health, though. I had been walking six miles to and from school several days a week and eating a healthier, mostly vegetarian diet, which may have contributed to some of the weight loss.

I had planned to stay in Africa for my one-year contract with WorldTeach, but now, six months in, I was sick and adrift, with no home to go back to. I had a return ticket to America in a few weeks, which was really a placeholder, since the schedule had only covered the next six months when I booked the ticket. The plan had been to change the date to cover the whole year when the new airline schedule was available, but now I had some decisions to make.

I didn't want to go home and impose my sick self on friends and family until my condo was available. Renting temporary lodgings would be expensive and probably depressing. All I could think of at the time was to go some-where nearby with good facilities and allow myself some time to heal and decide whether to take the scheduled flight home or come up with a new plan.

Victoria Falls wasn't exactly nearby. There was no direct flight there from Kigali and the quickest way was to fly almost 1,500 nautical miles south to Johannesburg, South Africa, and then 500 miles back up to Victoria Falls.

The last time I was there, in 1976, the country was still called Rhodesia and President Robert Mugabe was a guerrilla in the jungle. There had been little there besides the Victoria Falls Hotel, which opened in 1904, and the campground I had stayed at. I had spent some time at the hotel because my campground friends and I met and partied with a boisterous rugby team from Durban, South Africa, staying there. I remember the hotel as a slightly shabby but civilized refuge from the guerrilla war that threatened the country. There were very few tourists. In hindsight, the rugby team might have been the only people staying there, besides the staff. The hotel was closed up at night due to its proximity to the jungle, and the dimmed lights and blackout curtains gave it an eerie atmosphere.

Despite all that, I remembered that the place made me feel safe and happy, and that was the feeling I was looking to recover. Illness probably affected my clarity of thinking, because it feels odd now to describe safe and happy in terms of a place that had been in the middle of a bush war. But Victoria Falls had been a lodestone for me ever since I saw Spencer Tracy stand in front of the Falls in the 1939 movie, *Stanley and Livingstone*, and say, "Dr. Livingstone, I presume?" I couldn't resist an intrepid journalist, a doctor who went into the unknown to help humanity, and one of the most beautiful Wonders of the World. I think my emotions were at work more than my brain, because there were probably better places to go to recover.

I made the arrangements from Kigali, where I had good internet access. The Victoria Falls Hotel had been refurbished and was now rated five stars and out of my budget. I elected to stay next door at the Kingdom Hotel, which was under the same management, only a dozen years old, and $1,000 less for a week's stay. I had an upgraded room with king-sized bed, refrigerator, coffee pot, TV, and a good-sized balcony overlooking a stream and waterfall.

I hadn't had a television for about five months and was out of the habit. I had always been a news junkie, but I turned on CNN a few times during my stay and my brain could not stand the racket. I always turned it off after about five minutes. The only place I could get Wi-Fi was the hotel lobby. Despite being pretty unplugged from the modern world, I enjoyed the creature comforts of a lovely room decorated with stone tile and warm woods in soothing earth tones. The included huge buffet breakfast every morning helped my budget and my depleted body.

My first morning there, I sat on my large second-floor balcony after breakfast to read and relax. There was a gentle breeze and I heard a lot of rustling leaves in the big tree next to me. My head tilted up to the sky, enjoying the feel of the sun on my face, when I noticed five monkeys cavorting in the tree and adding to the noise. I enjoyed their antics for awhile until they started getting curious about me and jumped onto my balcony. That was enough to drive me inside to take a healing nap.

When I was there in 1976, there was little in the way of buildings in Victoria Falls. Now I was walking distance to many hotels, restaurants, shops, banks, and a supermarket. The grounds around the Falls that I used to walk all over freely now had tall fences restricting access, so it was hard to get good views of the Falls unless you paid thirty dollars to get in the National Park. Whatever decade, it's magical to walk along the trails around Victoria Falls, enjoying the drenching mist and colorful rainbows. The Falls are one of the Seven Natural Wonders of the World, twice as high and wider than Niagara Falls in the U.S.

The park entrance to the Falls was adjacent to my hotel, and it was one of my first ventures out during my "recovery" phase. The Falls were not in full flood and so not as spectacular as I had seen them before, but still wonderful. I saw several rainbows, which cheered me up.

On the way back to the park entrance, my energy was flagging so instead of walking back along the winding waterfall trail, I decided to take a shortcut to the gate and sit at one of the picnic tables there to eat the sack lunch the hotel had provided. The trail went through a grassy area with abundant trees. I saw no other people but noticed a baboon through the trees. After a few minutes, I saw several of them. I felt a little apprehensive but I kept walking, figuring a paved trail near the Park headquarters would be safe.

Suddenly, a large baboon dropped down from a branch right in front of me, flattened his ears and bared his long, sharp teeth. He only came up to my waist in height, but had long arms that reached for my bag lunch. My instinct was to pull the plastic bag away and stand my ground. The baboon's large canine teeth seemed to get bigger as he hissed and reached his long arms towards me. We had a brief tug of war with the bag until reason kicked in and warned me that fighting with a wild animal was not a good idea. I released the bag and the baboon quickly turned with his prize and loped away to his chattering friends.

Part of me felt like I had failed in the confrontation and should have stood up to him like I did to the bully teacher in Ngara, but I had the feeling the baboon was not going to back off. His teeth were definitely bigger than mine and I had felt the strength in his arms as we briefly fought for the bag. In hindsight, I thought about rabies and other unknown diseases a bite from those sharp teeth could deliver. It was worth a confrontation to keep my students safe, but a soggy turkey sandwich was not worth fighting for. I was relieved that I had come through unscathed.

∼

When the long bridge across the river near Victoria Falls opened in 1905, it was the highest bridge in the world. The Zambezi River serves as the border between Zimbabwe and Zambia. I couldn't walk all the way across the bridge to Zambia that day because I didn't have a visa, but there were many people in cars, trucks, and on foot making the crossing.

Thousands of bungee jumpers leap off the middle of the bridge every year. It made me really queasy to watch them do the 365-foot drop. It only took four seconds to go down but they had to stay upside-down for several minutes, waiting to be pulled up. I imagined that would cause quite a headache, especially with adrenaline making your blood rush.

I later read in a South African newspaper that soon after I was there, a female bungee jumper's line broke and she ended up in the river. Luckily, the crocodiles didn't find her, but she had to be airlifted to a hospital in South Africa for injuries sustained in the fall.

I had no money to buy lunch after the baboon stole mine, so I went to a nearby bank with an ATM. I was surprised that the machine spit out American dollars. Apparently the Zimbabwe currency was unstable and highly inflated, so many people used American dollars for transactions. Having a stack of twenty dollar bills after so long without them made me feel rich.

I eventually wandered over to the Victoria Falls Hotel for lunch. The interior public rooms of the hotel were decorated elegantly, with thick carpets, lavish draperies, polished dark wood, and small groupings of plush furniture. The walls featured large oil paintings of past royalty and many black and white pictures of the Royal family's stay there in 1947. I had seen the movie *The King's Speech* shortly before I left the U.S. and enjoyed viewing the happy faces of the real King George VI, his wife, and the young Princesses Elizabeth and Margaret. It was the first time an English Monarch brought his family on a major tour. They arrived via the Solent Flying Boat Service, which had a new route from Southampton, England to Johannesburg, South Africa. All the passengers disembarked and stayed overnight at the Victoria Falls Hotel. I was heartened to see the pictures showing the King and his family having an enjoyable visit. Five years after that visit, the King died of lung cancer and Elizabeth became Queen.

The hotel had a lovely terrace restaurant with a view of the hotel gardens, the bridge and the spray from the Falls. I considered getting the crocodile Caesar salad, but opted instead for a toasted chicken and bacon salad sandwich and a Zambezi beer, which were both delicious. Replete, I enjoyed feeling the sun on me as I felt the peace of the river and the Falls wash over me.

I felt like I was in the right place at the right time, but not ready to consider the future yet. I was thankful to be there, and just appreciating the moment was enough.

∼

After a few days of recuperation, I felt well enough to try a day safari. The hotel arranged for me and Mike, a black Jamaican who had settled in Dawson Creek, Canada, to be picked up by a Land Rover and driven to Chobe Marina Lodge on the Chobe River between Botswana and Namibia. We then boarded a boat for a morning cruise down the river.

I was able to sit and relax as we drifted by storks, fish eagles, kingfishers, egrets, African spoonbills, plovers, and herons perching on branches, standing balanced on one leg, or flying in the air. I love birds, but I was more enthusiastic about the animals I couldn't see at home, like Nile crocodiles, monitor lizards, vervet monkeys, hippos, cape buffalos, and water bucks.

"Look over there!" I shouted to Mike, excited to see some elephants rolling around in the mud on the river bank. They seemed to be playing, tossing mud at each other with their trunks before rolling onto their backs and wallowing in it.

"I read that the mud protects them from the heat and insects," said Mike. "Maybe we could use some."

"I'll stick with my lotions," I laughed.

Just past the wallowers, we saw a line of elephants of all sizes attached trunk to tail. The first one tentatively dipped into the water before rushing in with a huge splash, displacing the water enough that the spray reached our boat. The driver quickly backed up the boat and stopped so we drifted side-ways about fifty feet away. Somehow he kept us in that spot as we watched the line of elephants enter the water one by one until they were swimming. At one point a small baby elephant lost the connection and sunk under the water.

"Oh, no!" I cried. "The baby is going to drown!"

"I don't think so," said Mike. "See, the mother left the line and is going after him. It looks like she's using her trunk to grab him or push him. You can see the baby's small trunk sticking up out of the water."

We watched for a few terrible moments when the baby's trunk disappeared and there was no sign of it. The mother swam on, and we thought she had abandoned the baby for her own survival. As she reached the opposite shore, she pushed a small lump ahead of her. The lump turned out to be the baby elephant and he ran up the bank with his mother close behind him. The rest of the line of elephants, still attached, followed them up the bank.

"That was wonderful," I said, as I watched the elephants wander off. "It would be great to be a part of a community like that where everyone helps each other and no one is left behind."

"In my experience, most of the world is like that," Mike reflected. "You just have to find your tribe and avoid the bad apples. I thought I would miss my people in Jamaica, but I found a whole different group of people in the wilds of Canada who have become my new tribe. You have to be open to connecting with people."

I thought of the tightly bound, untrusting person I had been after my divorce. When the person who is supposed to be closest to you and have your back walks away, it's hard to trust someone else enough to let them step into that role. The time in Africa with mostly strangers was forcing me to depend on myself. I realized I had to trust myself before I could make healthy bonds with other people. I felt I had loosened up, but still had a long way to go.

We went back to the Marina Lodge for a nice buffet lunch before driving to the entrance to Chobe National Park for an afternoon game drive. The first animals we saw were a herd of impalas, small reddish colored antelopes with long elegant tapered horns.

"We call them the McDonalds of the Wilderness," joked Harry, our guide. "Fast food for the lions." He kept a running banter as we passed warthogs, buffaloes, tortoises, baboons, mongooses, and kudus. He got us out of the Land Rover to watch a dung beetle in the road comically trying to roll a ball of dung twice the size of his body.

"He puts the ball of dung in a hole and the female lays eggs on it," Harry explained. "The babies get their nutrients from the dung ball while they stay safely hidden in the hole."

Although we didn't see any giraffes or zebras in the National Park, there were some on the road back to the border. There were no fences, so the animals wandered in and out of the preserve. That freedom came with danger, though, as they became open targets for poachers, or someone just wanting a free dinner.

On the way back to the hotel, Mike told me his vacation was over and he was leaving Zimbabwe the next day. His main reason for coming to Africa had been to spend several weeks at Lion Walk, an NGO that was helping to reintroduce lions to the National Parks in Africa.

"I was looking for something different, and lions have always called to me," he declared. "I like their strength, their elegance, and their mastery of their environment. It makes me so sad that the lion population in Africa has dropped eighty to ninety percent in the last thirty years. At this rate, there will be no lions left outside of zoos."

Inspired by Mike's passion, I signed up for the Lion Walk, a fundraising activity that lets tourists walk with semi-tame lions at their preserve a few miles from town. The "walk" was only a half mile, so I figured I could handle it. I was tired of feeling wimpy. Our small group of six tourists met our guide, Hector, and watched a video about lions and how to interact with them.

"Lion Walk accustoms lions to people so they can raise money by having tourists walk with the lions," said Hector.

"The lions are well fed and protected, but we don't discourage their instinctive hunting behaviors. At age two, the lions are sent to another reserve where they are still watched and fed when needed, but left more on their own with no unnecessary human interaction. Any cubs they have are totally wild, and are eventually sent to various game reserves in Africa to bolster their lion populations. There are only a few lions in the project at a time, so it is a slow process."

We were each given long sticks and instructions on how to behave with the lions during the walk.

"If the lion gets aggressive in any way, you either tap him on the snout or put it between his teeth to distract him," explained Hector.

I stared dubiously at my stick, which was about two feet long and an inch in diameter. Not much of a defense against lion jaws, I thought. I couldn't imagine a lion settling down for me just because I hit him on the nose. More likely I'd be staring at his sharp teeth as he let out a roar and pounced on me. I started to feel that maybe getting close and personal with lions wasn't one of my better ideas.

Our group was introduced to the pair of lions we would be walking with. Initially, the lions were lying down and relaxing. One by one, we each got our photo ops showing us crouching down and petting them.

"Be very unthreatening," advised Hector. "Stroke them instead of patting them."

When it was my turn, I gave the lion some long strokes and pretended he was just a larger version of Poa. I never made eye contact with the big cat, since he was watching Hector. I thought an eye-to-eye connection with the creature would be more dangerous than actually touching him.

Guns were not allowed in the preserve, but two volunteers

joined us and several Africans walked with us at a more discreet distance. All carried bigger sticks than ours. The animals eventually got up and we started our walk. We were instructed to walk slowly with our stick between us and the animals. It felt like we were herding them, which seemed ridiculous.

"Don't let down your guard, because these lions are still half-wild," advised Hector. "Last year, an impala ran past and both lions took off after it and killed it. We don't interfere with their natural instincts. That's why we tell you to walk slow. They are naturally attracted to things running away from them."

There was no way I was going to run. By the time we finished our half-mile walk, I felt more comfortable, but still guarded. We were put into a wooden building at the end of the walk before they "released" the animals by some unknown signal.

I thought of the lioness I had seen in the brambles in Chobe. She had put herself in that cage-like environment. Like her, we were in the building for protection, but free to leave. The lions on the preserve could race after game but would be killed if they tried to leave its confines. They were half-wild, but also half-tame. They were used to people, and might kill somebody if they were hungry and not fed regularly. That made them too great a threat to roam free. For the rest of their lives, they would be slaves to the tourist trade.

We could purchase videos of our walk, though I never saw the photographer. The guide and volunteers had been happy to take pictures of us with our personal cameras. So I do have proof that I walked with a lion and a lioness. Somehow it doesn't feel like I did though. Maybe I was just too afraid to process it. But I was proud that I had faced my fear and completed the walk.

By this time I was about a week into my "recovery." The mostly Western diet I was eating might have been less healthy than all those fruits and vegetables in Ngara, but maybe the quantity mattered more than the quality. Besides fruits and vegetables, I was eating meat or eggs twice a day and drinking plenty of water.

I finally felt ready for something more active. I decided against whitewater rafting because it required going up and down a huge mountain with steps and no handrails to get to the river. This would be difficult for me normally, and more so because my recent health issues made my sense of balance worse. I had fallen down more than once.

Instead, I went canoeing on the Zambezi River between Zimbabwe and Zambia. There were national parks on both sides, so it felt like complete wilderness except for a few isolated resorts along the shores. My companions on the tour were an Australian couple and their three daughters, ages eight to eighteen. Obit, one of two guides, instructed us to sit with two people in each canoe. I shared one with Obit, which left a child for each parent and the other guide.

Our canoes glided around the many islands in the river. A few sections had small rapids and whirlpools, which made the canoes spin a bit. There was no way to avoid getting wet, but the water felt wonderfully warm. The temperature was hotter than in Ngara or Kigali, ranging from 75 to 85 degrees.

We saw lots of hippos, which are known as the most dangerous animal in the water in Africa, since they kill more people than any other. Usually they just stood placidly in the water with only their eyes, ears, and the tops of their heads showing. Obit told us groups with baby hippos would be especially dangerous to go near, but that he knew the ones to avoid.

Suddenly one of the hippos we were watching opened his huge mouth wide and showed all his teeth.

"That's a sign of aggression," yelled Obit. "Row faster!"

The other canoes swiftly paddled downriver, leaving Obit and me in the rear. I kept looking back and it seemed like the hippo was gaining steadily on us.

"Row faster," Obit yelled again.

My arms burned as I dug deeper with my paddle, trying to make the boat go as fast as possible. The hippo was only a few feet away when we came to some rapids. The hippo stopped and stared at us as the turbulent water sped us away and left him behind.

"There is more than one way for water to save people," I reflected. But then I thought of tidal waves and floods and decided water was essentially neutral, but with big swings to both sides of the balance. It was life saving, but it could also kill, so it had to be respected.

Later, I splurged on a fifteen-minute helicopter ride over the Falls. The clouds had given way to blue sky, and I had wonderful views. It was not flood season yet, when the spray could shoot up well over a thousand feet, but it was still impressive. Although Victoria Falls is not the highest or widest waterfall in the world, it is considered the largest, with the biggest volume of water cascading down the mile-wide face.

I felt a sense of wonder that I had the privilege to see such a thing, and it made me think back on my six-month journey to get to that place. I recognized that I had come to Africa weak, damaged, and with low self-esteem. I had been a caregiver for years, both at home and at work. In my career as a nurse, I had absorbed the emotional trauma of hundreds of patients and their loved ones who faced devastating problems like cancer, heart attacks, and horrible accidents as I tried to help them heal. At times, helping them deal with the American medical system was a trauma in itself.

At home, I was a peacemaker and avoided conflict, striving for calm and reason over anger and strife. In my community, I was involved in school, political, and environmental issues, some of them very contentious. Over time, all of these strands pulled at me, making me wrap myself tighter to maintain sanity and outward control. Everything crashed with the divorce and job loss. I felt inadequate, unlovable and alone, with my support systems shredded. Anxiety ruled me, and running away to Africa was akin to the child in me running away from home.

But Africa offered me a reset. I knew nobody and was responsible for no one. All my decisions were mine alone. I had to pick myself up off the ground and start anew. It was past time to release the old, toxic patterns and find the power within me.

I thought of my time in Africa. Surely a "weak" person could not have handled what I had been through in the last six months. That person would have been on a flight home the first week. There had been many highs, but also debilitating lows. I felt physically stronger than when I arrived at Victoria Falls and realized I was mentally stronger, as well. The passiveness had been replaced by the personal power I needed to survive. I reflected on all I had done in just the past week, with hippos, baboons, and a helicopter. I was living far outside my comfort zone, and loving it.

I sat on a bench and watched the massive water flow cascade over the falls. A rainbow arched over the gorge, its shimmering colors like a beacon of welcome. It reinforced my sense of connection to Africa. I was not ready to go home.

When I got back to the hotel, I booked a Christmas safari

as a reward to myself for persevering this far. I had suffered physically, but getting out of the daily grind back home had forced me to trust and depend on myself. I felt I was growing as a person but had further to go. One step at a time felt like enough, for now. I had a plane ticket as an escape hatch, if I needed it.

My last evening there, I went to the Boma Restaurant for a great buffet of all the food I never knew I wanted to try, with lots of wild game, both grilled and in salads. I ate kudu, eland, warthog, guinea fowl, and impala, as well as fish and chicken. Forced vegetarianism had made me into a rampant carnivore, but I wasn't far gone enough to try the Mopani worms.

There was a demonstration by native dancers and singers before the staff handed out African drums and a Drum Master instructed the guests to get a good rhythm going. We started slowly but gradually stepped up the beat. I felt the rhythm wash through me as I energetically pounded on the drums.

I had no conscious thoughts. I smiled. I laughed. I stood. I swayed. It seemed like my miniscule bits of African DNA were resurging and making themselves known. I felt the ropes that had been tying me down burst free and connect me with the Drum Master, the other dancers, the music, and the universe.

As I danced, a long-forgotten feeling of freedom swept over me and welcomed me home.

...to be continued

AFTERWORD

Thank you so much for reading my book.

I hope you enjoyed reading about my journey. It covers a bad time in my life but I hope it might help others to see that life is a series of ebbs and flows. We hang on for the ride, but the worst thing is to get stuck in a rut. Sometimes you have to give a little push one way or the other to get past the depression, low self-esteem, unhealthy relationships, procrastination or whatever is holding you back from finding your best life. Traveling in Africa was definitely a push for me, but you can probably find a similar catalyst a lot closer to home if you look.

Please find my book on Amazon.com and leave an honest review. I would love to hear what you think, as it may help guide me in future writings. This book only covers half of my year in Africa so there's more to come! You can find out more about my journey, including pictures, on my blog at footloosemary.com.

ACKNOWLEDGMENTS

A book is like a boat.

Thanks to R.E. Vance for identifying water as the theme and underpinning that floats the boat, Vanessa Vlahakis for making it shipshape, and all the great people at Self-Publishing School who had patience with this wobbly sailor and helped guide it home.

ABOUT THE AUTHOR

Mary Morrison got the travel bug early.

She haunted the history and travel sections of her local public library in California and wrote to the New Zealand consulate at age 12 to ask about immigrating there. They sent her a poster, which stayed on her bedroom wall for several years.

Mary has traveled to over 100 countries, seeking connection to people and places. She currently lives in the beautiful Blue Ridge mountains. Learn more about Mary's journeys at footloosemary.com